PRAISE FOR *THE GENEROSITY CRISIS*

"*The Generosity Crisis* is a powerful analysis of the changing dynamic in society related to giving, philanthropy and brands. The need for a more radical connection between people and organizations may sound like a simple concept; however, it is incredibly complicated and when done properly will change the trajectory of generosity for future generations. Brian, Nathan and Michael have painted a compelling picture for what is behind effective communication in today's world."

—Chris Foster, CEO, Omnicom PR Group

"As someone who is dedicated to helping nonprofit organizations leverage the benefits of technology, I'm thrilled to see the authors of *The Generosity Crisis* bring to light many of the critical issues facing philanthropy and nonprofits today. I have seen the positive impact modern technology can have when leveraged for good on accelerating mission outcomes. Harnessing data, cloud, AI and machine learning enables personalization at scale, creating powerful connections and the ability to drive results. I celebrate the practical guidelines and actionable insights provided that will inspire philanthropic leaders towards a new vision for how they prioritize their time and resources to deliver on mission!"

—Allyson Fryhoff, managing director, Nonprofit Business, Amazon Web Services

"We don't have an inequality crisis, a climate crisis or an economic crisis, we have a leadership crisis, driven by vested interests and their selfishness, apathy and greed. Brian and Nathan set out a simple but often overlooked truth: that generosity and connection must be central in our response."

—Paul Polman, business leader, campaigner and coauthor of *Net Positive*

"We humans are blessed with an instinct for generosity. But the structures of the modern world can suppress that instinct. We're isolated from each other—and that isolation matters not just for our mental health, but for society's health. When we look closely, we see that generosity is not just a beautiful emotion, it is a fuel for our economy and a foundation for our communities."

—Jacob Harold, former CEO of GuideStar, author of *The Toolbox*

"Being a young woman who comes from a different part of the world (India) and having lived in the United States of America for only a short period of time, I was unaware of generosity crisis in America. As I turned over each page into this incredible journey, the facts and information that appeared before me absolutely helped me to find the answers to the many questions I had about generosity in general. My time in America was made easier with the help of this book, *The Generosity Crisis*, by Nathan Chappell, Brian Crimmins, and Michael Ashley. I can't imagine how challenging it would be to tackle this topic. Thank you for your thoughtfulness and sharing with me this great book of knowledge."

—Harnaaz Sandhu, Miss Universe 2021

"The WHO Foundation is witness to the transformative power of philanthropy every day. Individuals are supporting the work to stop diseases, provide basic medicines and ensure children and families around the world have equal access to a healthy life. *The Generosity Crisis* shines a bright spotlight on the unimaginable consequences to humanity should philanthropy erode. But with awareness comes hope. The authors charge the reader to evaluate their responsibility in the world to link arms and provide a healthier and more equitable future for everyone."

—Anil Soni, CEO of The WHO Foundation, Geneva

THE GENEROSITY
CRISIS

THE GENEROSITY
CRISIS

The Case for **RADICAL CONNECTION**
to Solve Humanity's Greatest Challenges

NATHAN
CHAPPELL

BRIAN
CRIMMINS

MICHAEL
ASHLEY

WILEY

Published by John Wiley & Sons, Inc., Hoboken, New Jersey.
Published simultaneously in Canada.

For general information on our other products and services or for technical support, please contact our Customer Care Department within the United States at (800) 762–2974, outside the United States at (317) 572–3993 or fax (317) 572–4002.

Wiley also publishes its books in a variety of electronic formats. Some content that appears in print may not be available in electronic formats. For more information about Wiley products, visit our web site at www.wiley.com.

Library of Congress Cataloging-in-Publication Data is Available:

ISBN 9781394150571 (Cloth)
ISBN 9781394150588 (ePub)
ISBN 9781394150595 (ePDF)

Cover Design: Nathan Chappell
Cover Image: © lidiia/Adobe Stock

SKY10036129_092222

For those that strive to make the world a better place, one connection at a time.

CONTENTS

INTRODUCTION

The future of generosity in America is not guaranteed.
—*The Generosity Commission (2020)*

Uninterrupted, those who engage in traditional philanthropy will cease to exist in 49 years. This is a problem of monumental proportions. If the love of money is the root of evil, generosity is the salve that makes the world go around. The challenge is most of the public doesn't realize charitable giving underpins so much of our daily lives and thus it operates without much consideration as to how their personal connection to generosity has immeasurable consequences.

Providing untold benefits, charitable giving offers relief and assistance to the poor and disadvantaged as well as the victims of wars and catastrophes. It also supplies shelter, educational resources, medical cures, advances, and care for our most vulnerable. Besides aiding with environmental causes, generosity contributes to the economy, especially concerning the arts and culture. A 2019 report by the Center for Civil Society Studies at Johns Hopkins University states that nonprofits account for roughly 1 in 10 jobs in the US private workforce, with total employees numbering 12.3 million in 2016.

Despite all this, too many people don't realize the dangers should philanthropy continue its downward trajectory. Today's hospitals, food pantries, homeless shelters, colleges, museums, and the arts would all suffer—if not outright vanish. We had a preview of this risk in 2021. Activists and other concerned influencers worried that charitable donations would decline due to economic contraction from COVID-19. But then something surprising happened. When the dust settled, it turned out $484.85 billion was raised.

Superficially, this seemed good, especially because this figure surpassed the prior year of giving: $471.44 billion. But charity is not outpacing gross domestic product (GDP) and the mix of who gives to charity reflects a growing wealth disparity. Instead, charitable giving continues to increase at the same rate as the economy (~2.1% of the GDP, where it has remained for the past 40 years). Also, fewer US households are participating in traditional philanthropy toward charitable causes.

This means if it weren't for a handful of very generous megadonors such as MacKenzie Scott, who has given away more than $12 billion since 2019, total philanthropy in America would have decreased significantly over the past few years. Of course, all too often well-meaning pundits celebrate growth for growth's sake, instead of looking deeper to understand *who* accounts for such beneficence. These days, fewer people are giving and those who do give . . . *give less*. The share of households donating to charity has been decreasing annually and fell to its lowest level in decades—just 49.6%—portending even fewer donations in the coming years. Worse, as more people leave faith-based organizations, the engine for so much community-minded generosity, we can expect charitable giving to fall even further.

But the news isn't all bad.

Despite so many reports about how technology is dividing people, novel opportunities exist to use such advancements for myriad humanitarian purposes. We live in an era of personalization and customization, which translates to the concept of a "precision" approach to consumerism. Why not employ the same meticulousness in the service of innovating how charities prospect donors? Since 2017, coauthor Nathan Chappell has led efforts to leverage cutting-edge artificial intelligence and big data to enable organizations to better understand the true motivations of generosity and identify why some people align with a specific cause.

At the heart of such efforts is a disruption of conventional thinking toward generosity. For too long, nonprofits and the like have relied on a person's *wealth* as the key metric for predicting someone's willingness to give. But a limited approach is at the root the crisis in US giving. Instead, tomorrow's nonprofits can achieve better fundraising outcomes by measuring individuals' depth of *affinity* to worthwhile causes. Empowered by this insight, they can (re)focus their efforts toward cultivating deep, sustaining relationships by fostering what we term *Radical Connection*. Also, collaborating with progressive for-profit companies serving the public good in essential ways can help flip the giving script.

Fortunately, for the first time in history, it's possible to dramatically increase precision and personalization in services and soft industries using big data and adaptive and cognitive computing powers. Marrying digital and analog activities, we can better connect with mission-aligned people and groups. Better yet, by emphasizing innovative ways of giving, including volunteering, crowdfunding, mentoring, and other forms of service-ship, we can especially teach the younger generation about new ways of giving back. Beyond exploring these key strategies in the following pages, we will show how a confluence of nonprofits, for-profit companies, governmental entities, and NGOs are trailblazing fresh and exciting paths toward greater giving for the benefit of all.

To get there we need to look at this issue with fresh eyes. Philanthropy at its core is really about connection, not money. We will highlight this idea throughout the book. In fact, the ancient Greek meaning of the word, "for love of humankind," has nothing to do with money. Yet too often, philanthropy is thought of as something only wealthy people do. In truth, giving money, offering advocacy, or providing volunteerism constitute the outward expression of *connection*. And yet, what was once first nature to many legacy nonprofit causes—building and fostering deep authentic relationships transcending generations—has been replaced by surface-level transactions, leaving an unbalanced relationship between mission and benefactor.

This very imbalance and the transactional nature of many modern charitable organizations is at the heart of our Generosity Crisis. Generosity as a civic responsibility is at an inflection point, requiring a positive outlook and new modes of thinking to reverse negative trends toward giving back. By doing so, we stand a chance at solving some of the world's most pressing issues. Transforming a depressing crisis into a pivotal opportunity, let's imagine a brighter future in which once disparate groups and individuals regain their sense of Radical Connection and commitment, resulting in greater abundance and a renewal of goodwill.

Last, as we dive deep to understand the root causes of the Generosity Crisis, let's fully embrace what's at stake and explore what's needed to reverse the downward giving paradigm. We hope this book inspires you to think about your personal views on the relationship between generosity and connection and to create an open dialogue about the changing definition of philanthropy.

PART I

OUR PROBLEM

CHAPTER 1

What Would Happen if Everyone Stopped Giving?

Kelley woke up soaked. Nine months pregnant, her water broke at dawn. In seconds, her husband gathers their stuff, and they rush out the door. They arrive at the hospital to receive the shock of their lives. The doors are locked. A sign reads: "Closed until further notice."

Across town, Cameron goes to his mailbox excited to receive grant approval to study the effects of dwindling coral reefs. Three years into his Ph.D. program, Cameron has poured his heart into composing a research grant submission to net $5 million. He even put off proposing to his girlfriend so he can relocate to Australia to work on reversing the reefs' rapid decay. To Cameron's dismay, he receives a rejection letter from his university informing him all future research is being halted.

At a nearby zoo, Maria sheds tears, but not for the job she just lost. She cries because she knows what will happen when her employer closes. Once a sanctuary for endangered species, the zoo will have to sell its animals to the highest bidder.

At this same moment, lifelong curator Pierre slumps deeper into his swivel chair. Watching footage from CCTV cameras all over the building, he sees priceless works of art carted off for auction. In weeks, Impressionist works, some hundreds of years old, will be bought by private collectors. He sighs, recalling a line from the Indiana Jones movies, "It belongs in a museum!"

Down the street, a sad pastor tells a family of three they can no longer receive food from his pantry. Two little kids and their mom relied on this benevolence ever since she lost her job last year. No more. The program is ending. So is the church that funded its operations.

This is just the beginning. Before long the following examples describe what can happen:

- Clinics stop providing free health care screenings.

- Starved of funding, theaters, operas, and symphonies cease performing.

- Homeless shelters shutter, leaving the displaced to fend for themselves.

- Welfare services terminate, exposing at-risk children to abuse.

- Scientific exploration grinds to a halt at observatories and labs.

Imagine you woke up one day to a world in which all generosity ended. The described outcomes are but a small sampling of what you could expect, and not so far-fetched. Generosity in America is on a disastrous trajectory. The year 2019 represented the lowest giving level since Giving USA (GUSA) began compiling national philanthropic statistics 40 years ago. According to a report by the Indiana University Lilly Family School of Philanthropy, in 2000 an estimated 66% (one-third) of Americans gave to charity. By 2014 this figure had decreased to 55%, and in 2016 it had fallen to just 53%. The past three years were even worse. At present, less than half (49.6%) of Americans give to charities. The nation is becoming less giving every year, and it doesn't take a degree in mathematics to see where this trend is going or economic proficiency to project the negative consequences.

Unfortunately, the public doesn't hear the Generosity Crisis message enough. If at all. Instead, people are led to believe their contributions are inconsequential and that charity, and the services provided through generosity, will continue as they always have. Nothing could be further from the truth. "This belief of not having enough to give to make a difference is similar to the argument some people make when it comes to voting," explains Sarah Ford, marketing director at America's Charities. "But try telling a senator who wins by 18 votes that your vote doesn't matter and I promise they'll give you an earful." Without charitable gifts, so many societal mainstays and benefits we take for granted will vanish. Let's review examples by category.

HOSPITALS

GUSA reports the health industry received charitable donations of $42.12 billion in 2020. This figure is essential to the functioning of hospitals throughout the nation, from caring for the sick, providing ancillary services to support families through their treatments, to research and development for novel care practices and cures. As an association that surveys the health care landscape, Incredible Health documents as of September 21, 2021, "the two main types of hospitals in the United States are nonprofit and for-profit hospitals. According to the American Hospital Association, 76% of community hospitals are nonprofit."

This means should philanthropy cease, Kelley's nightmare scenario is not at all unrealistic. Thousands of local nonprofit hospitals would close, forcing patients into government-run or for-profit medical centers with all the high costs and lack of options you might expect. Many health care jobs would also vanish overnight, along with critical research and development. With fewer hospitals and health care professionals, vast lines to access care would resemble those of third-world countries.

COLLEGES AND UNIVERSITIES

Higher education received $71.34 billion in donations in 2020, again according to GUSA. There is little debate that tuition costs are astronomical, having risen at five times the inflation rate for the past 50 years, according to the College Board. We can scarcely imagine what would happen if alumni and other stakeholders stopped giving. To illustrate the problem, consider 2019's under-graduate tuition cost $55,046 at University of Notre Dame, coauthor Nathan's alma mater. After grants, scholarships, and other subsidies, much of which is funded though charitable gifts to the university, this figure drops to a more manageable $30,536.

Also, it should be noted, colleges offer financial lifeblood to their communities. Take South Bend, the city surrounding Notre Dame. According to citytowninfo.com, "South Bend's diversified economy primarily consists of education, wholesale and retail trade, healthcare, and government. Notre Dame University is the city's largest employer and has a significant impact on the local economy. The university also adds to the economy by part-nering with local companies for research and development projects."

If colleges at large lost their donations, most students could no longer afford to earn degrees. Likewise, the businesses and people who depend on the commerce, not to mention research and medical resources contingent on their existence, would suf-fer. Academic projects, such as studying diminishing coral reefs pursued by the Camerons of the world, would never get off the ground.

COVID-19 gave us a taste of such a disaster when so many students found themselves unable to continue their studies. As Jessica Dickler reported for CNBC in June 2020, "With millions of Americans now out of work, one expense is suddenly out of reach for many: higher education. More than half, or 56%, of college students say they can no longer afford their tuition tab, according to a survey by OneClass, which polled more than 10,000 current freshmen, sophomores and juniors from 200-plus colleges and universities across the country."

Zoos

GUSA reported that individuals gave $16.14 billion to environmental and animal causes in 2020. Some people hold a limited view of zoos as places to stare at lions and tigers and maybe pet a chinchilla. But these facilities do much to protect and sustain nature, especially endangered species. As Amber Wyard explains for lemurconservationnetwork.org, "Although recreation is still an important focus for zoos, they now place a lot of value on education, research, and conservation."

To this point and according to Association of Zoos & Aquariums, more than 230 top zoos and aquariums "provide safe habitats, medical care, and a nurturing environment for their animals." Using the funds they receive from donations, they breed and save animals, including gorillas in Rwanda, lemurs in Madagascar, and vultures in Southern Tanzania.

If people stop believing in the virtues of giving and halt their philanthropic monies, these conservation efforts would cease, curtailing progress made in the last 100 years; it's also likely many animals would end up in private hands. We can expect less accountability should this occur, leading to dramatic increases in animal trafficking as depicted in the disturbing 2020 documentary *Tiger King*.

MUSEUMS

According to Sotheby's Institute of Art, three categories of revenue support nonprofit museums:

- Charitable contributions
- Program services, such as ticket admissions
- Earned income, typically via merchandising

Of the three sources, the first category provides the lion's share of funding, accounting "for over half of a museums' revenue at an industry standard of around 60%." Should philanthropy end, it would decimate museums' fundraising model. After all, GUSA reported the arts, culture, and humanities organizations received $19.47 billion in donations in 2020.

Loss of museums would devastate not just creatives but also society. In a 2015 interview with *Alliance Magazine*, Sir Nicholas Serota, director of the UK's Tate Modern, reflected on how philanthropy enables the arts, specifically the world's most popular museum of modern and contemporary art. "None of Tate's expansion or the growth in audiences from 1.75 million to 7.75 million over 20 years would have been possible without a partnership between secure public funding. . . . One of our first significant donations for Tate Modern came from a man not noted for his enthusiasm for modern art. He was motivated to give because he recognized the need for London to have a museum of international contemporary art and he knew that cultural investment in a relatively poor part of London could transform the area economically and socially."

Lacking such generosity, we could expect to see chains on doors and vacant museums as their business model collapsed. Like the zoo debacle, art pieces, both modern and antiquated, would be auctioned to bidders. No longer could the public enjoy their cultural birthright. In this scenario, even the *Mona Lisa* would depart the Louvre, undoubtedly snatched up by a rich collector.

British journalist A. A. Gill helps to explain what we stand to lose: "If the world were to end tomorrow and we could choose to save only one thing as the explanation and memorial to who we were, then we couldn't do better than the Natural History Museum, although it wouldn't contain a single human. The systematic Linnaean order, the vast inquisitiveness and range of collated knowledge and beauty would tell all that is the best of us."

HUMAN SERVICES

Our scenario depicting the closure of shelters is not fantastical. GUSA reports the broad category of human services received $65.14 billion in donations in 2020. According to Feeding America, food insecurity in America is a pervasive issue, with 38 million adults and 12 million children undernourished, not knowing where they will get their next meal. Meanwhile, homelessness continues unabated. As of 2022, estimates from two key sources of data—the US Department of Housing and Urban Development Point-in-Time Count and the National Center for Education Statistics Count of Students—puts the number of people lacking permanent housing between 600,000 and 1.5 million, of which 33% are families with children.

In 2019, the Council of Economic Advisers sought to explain the crisis in a paper titled *The State of Homelessness in America*. "Approximately 65 percent are found in homeless shelters, and the other 35 percent—just under 200,000—are found unsheltered on our streets (in places not intended for human habitation, such as sidewalks, parks, cars, or abandoned buildings)."

A 1:1 relationship exists between the level at which people give and the homelessness crisis at large. Sadly, we've grown accustomed to seeing long lines to shelters and foodbanks. Although government funding plays a role in addressing this challenge, it cannot fix the crisis on its own. Human service issues, such as food insecurity and homelessness, can only be solved via public-private partnerships, underpinned by the generosity of individuals who believe in supporting their fellow brothers and sisters.

Zeroing in on one organization, The National Association of Free & Charitable Clinics, we gain a deeper sense of the assistance it provides, especially for those requiring medical care. Self-described as "the only nonprofit 501(c)(3) organization whose mission is solely focused on the issues and needs of the medically underserved throughout the United States," it serves the poor, especially those in need of health services, via a robust network of 1,400 free and charitable clinics and pharmacies.

In 2020 the NAFC received $286 million in donated medications and supplies. Without critical monies and product donations, we could expect the closure of many free clinics supporting underserved populations by offering free or reduced cost services:

- Diabetes programs
- Dental cleanings
- Eye exams and glasses
- Cancer screenings
- Mental health and psychiatric services

By no means is this list exhaustive. If we consider only the health challenges we have encountered over the years, not to mention our friends and family members, we can appreciate the issues facing vulnerable individuals who experience higher rates of serious health conditions. Also, loss of shelters and medical facilities will unduly affect children, especially those lacking stability and/or a guardian. This problem compounds for nonlegal citizens, poised to the bear the brunt of the pain should these facilities and amenities vanish from lack of funding.

PERFORMING ARTS

This sector depends on generosity from patrons and the public. Just as museums remind us of our history through appreciating paintings and exhibits, the performing arts connect us to our higher selves by entertaining and inspiring. Or as Investing in Communities (IIC) puts it so eloquently, "Arts and culture charities is a broad term for organizations that exist to promote and develop artistic expression. They preserve our cultural heritage through media including exhibitions and performances. . . . Arts and culture charities encourage education and appreciation of numerous artistic disciplines including painting, sculpture, writing, photography, puppetry, film, theater, opera, dance, and music. By supporting one of these organizations, you are showing your support for the creative expression of human experience."

As IIC makes clear, a fulfilling life encompasses more than just keeping a roof over one's head. By stanching the blood of the performing arts, we cut ourselves off from what it means to be human, losing out on a full spectrum of artistic expression so vital to the experience of being. We take these things for granted at present. As a civilized nation we expect they will always be there for us, but they could slip away if we are not careful.

TECHNOLOGY

The COVID-19 pandemic revealed in technicolor horror the vulnerability of our global community. Within weeks, a deadly virus spread from one nation to engulf the world. Yet, this outbreak differed from past scourges. People could turn to key medical innovations. Some, such as vaccines and treatments, emerged in record time to counter the disease's effects and keep us connected. A variety of teleconferencing solutions, for instance, acted as a godsend, especially for businesses and schools, enabling their functioning, albeit in a remote capacity. "The nonprofit world was profoundly changed by COVID—but there was a silver lining," says Maria Clark, executive vice president of partnerships at GoodUnited, a longtime nonprofit leader personally affected by the pandemic. She said the following in a 2021 article for Unite.AI: "Innovation became a necessity, not a luxury, which stimulated the adoption of new strategies and partnerships in order to continue fueling the important work nonprofits are expected to deliver."

Those affected by the Black Death or bubonic plague couldn't expect such reprieve. But innovation costs money. It requires benefactors who believe in science. In their review of Evan S. Michelson's 2020 book, *Philanthropy and the Future of Science and Technology for Issues in Science and Technology*, columnists Adam Millsap and Neil Chilson trumpet this cause. Specifically, they connect the dots between charitable giving and recent technological feats. "In the book's most compelling section, Michelson discusses the evolution of foundation giving over the 20th century. . . . For example, The Rockefeller Foundation funded research in cellular and molecular biology with the purpose of eliminating disease, and indeed that work helped to eradicate hookworm and yellow fever. Michelson makes a very brief mention of The Rockefeller Foundation's support for the agricultural Green Revolution, which dramatically increased the world's food supply and arguably preserved and advanced democracy during the Cold War."

Now, what might happen should this investment in our future vanish? We could expect any of the following:

- Significant increases in the digital divide
- Less funding for disease and wellness research
- Severe limitations on climate change initiatives
- Diminution of advancements in AI and computer applications
- Decrease in space exploration
- Curtailed WIFI, laptops, and phone distribution to the needy

As this list shows, daily life relies on philanthropy. Much of what we have come to expect and enjoy comes from the kindness of others. Faith-based organizations especially rely on donations, topping GUSA's list of contributions at $131 billion for 2020. Without such generosity, not only would churches close, the broad swath of ancillary benefits those churches provide would disappear, including social services such as food pantries.

So far, we have discussed various categories as potential victims of a giving chopping block. Yet even this depressing portrait doesn't go far enough. Another emergent problem looms. As the ongoing supply chain crisis reveals, we live in an integrated global economy. Events no longer happen in isolation; rather, they have far-reaching, *systemic* impacts.

A good example of such economic dependence can be found in Ningbo. When China locked down this industrial port in

January 2022 for a COVID-19 outbreak, it didn't just affect the local economy. As the third largest global container port, the closure ramifications were felt as far away as the US, affecting consumer delivery times and incomes of truck drivers. Revealingly, an entire ecosystem of businesses, nonprofits, and individuals interact with what we may call the Generosity Economy.

Here are some critical statistics as of 2021:

- More than 10 million nonprofits and nongovernmental organizations exist worldwide (NPAction.org).

- Roughly 1.8 million 501(c)(3) organizations are based in the US, including 501(c)(3) public charities, private foundations, and a variety of membership and professional organizations (Nonprofit Trends and Impact, 2021).

- Nonprofits account for 5% to 10% of the national economy and 10% of American employment (*Stanford Social Innovation Review*).

- The US nonprofit sector employs nearly 12 million people, making it the third largest employment industry, behind retail and manufacturing (Johns Hopkins University Center for Civil Society Studies).

To illustrate but a fraction of the labyrinthine workings of so many interrelated stakeholders and how they might be affected by the crisis, consider one more stat from IBISWorld. "New York (1,523 businesses), California (1,186 businesses) and Texas (769 businesses) are the States with the most number of Community Housing & Homeless Shelters businesses in the US."

Now, what might happen should so many businesses fold due to a philanthropy cessation? It would not only devastate those who own and/or work at these companies but also would harm their families and the people who depend on them (not to mention the individuals who benefit from their charitable works). But the problem wouldn't stop there. Because we now live and work in an integrated global economy, deleterious effects would spread. If just one of the 769 businesses in Texas supplying shelters went under, it could wreak havoc with vendors. This could mean cancelled contracts for a host of tangential services, from building to transportation to food supply.

In short, negative ripple effects from annual decreases in US generosity have created this systemic Generosity Crisis. Left unchecked, it will touch *all* our lives, no matter where we exist in the ecosystem.

THE TRUTH ABOUT PHILANTHROPY

Countering a crisis of such intricate and profound proportions requires us to consider the issue with fresh eyes. We began our discussion by depicting how everyday people might be affected should generosity cease. Although dramatic, it's a very possible scenario should giving levels continue falling at their current trajectory. In the chapters to come we will explore the reasons people are giving less and how to counter this challenge. For now, making real, sustainable change requires greater awareness. After all, how can we ever hope to combat decreased giving without knowing the underlying problems?

The truth is, we cannot. Worse than ignorance, misconceptions plague this subject, obscuring perceptions. To turn things around we must disabuse people of many limiting beliefs. We must shatter five damaging, wrongheaded myths once and for all.

Myth 1: Philanthropy Is a Recent Phenomenon

The average misinformed person may believe philanthropy began with the era of giving from billionaires such as Bill Gates, Warren Buffet, and Oprah Winfrey, all members of the so-called Good Club. This is false. The origins of giving predate Jesus. Aristotle, the Greek philosopher, wrote about this subject in *Nicomachean Ethics*: "To give away money is an easy matter and in any man's power. But to decide to whom to give it, and how large, and when, and for what purpose and how, is neither in every man's power nor an easy matter." Essentially, he was demonstrating the point that although the concept of giving away money appears easy at face value, the *act* of generosity is highly nuanced with several barriers that may easily dissuade someone with good intentions from following through with giving.

"Most people who spend too much, as it is said, both take what is not right and are cheap because of that. They become greedy because they want to spend but cannot do this easily because their funds quickly escape them. They are therefore compelled to procure from elsewhere. In addition, because they don't think at all about nobility of action, they take from everywhere. They desire to give, and it makes no difference how or where to them. For this reason, their giving is not liberal because the gifts are not noble or given for nobility's sake, nor in the way that is correct. Sometimes they make those rich who ought to be poor and they will give nothing to those humble in character, but they provide much to their flatterers and those who please them."

Skipping ahead at warp speed, let's acknowledge noteworthy highlights on the generosity timeline to show US philanthropy is anything but new.

1636: Harvard College (originally named The New College) begins in the Massachusetts Bay Colony after John Harvard, a minister, bequeaths his library and half his estate to the university on death. Successive private schools of the religious variety will follow, including Yale and Princeton.

1700s: Informed by decades of civic involvement, Benjamin Franklin creates America's first subscription library in 1731 as well as a volunteer fire organization, a fire insurance association, and the Philadelphia Academy in 1751, which later becomes the University of Pennsylvania.

1860s: To raise funds and supplies for the Union's efforts to win the Civil War, northern women organize fundraising events. Much of their efforts go toward the U.S. Sanitary Commission. Women, such as Dorothea Dix and Clara Barton, volunteer by nursing sick and wounded soldiers in local hospitals and even on battlefields.

1881: Founded by the same Barton, the Red Cross launches as a volunteer organization, conducting some of the first domestic and overseas disaster relief efforts, even aiding the US military during the Spanish-American War.

1910: Steel industrialist Andrew Carnegie donates $10 million to fund the Carnegie Endowment for International Peace. Carnegie writes a charter outlining what his group shall do after ending armed conflict. "When the establishment of universal peace is attained, the donor provides that the revenue shall be devoted to the banishment of the next most degrading evil or evils, the suppression of which would most advance the progress, elevation, and happiness of man."

Unfortunately for Carnegie and the planet, World War I started four years later. Still, as these examples attest, philanthropy has been alive and well in the US for almost 400 years.

Myth 2: Philanthropy Mostly Comes from Rich White Men

Speaking of the Gates, Buffets, and Carnegies, a common belief persists that only this subgroup gives. Though it's true that the likes of the Rockefellers have donated vast fortunes in service of humanity, they are not alone. If it wasn't for MacKenzie Scott donating more than $12 billion since 2019, average giving as a function of our GDP would not have stayed at approximately 2%—where it's hovered for the past four decades. (This statistic is according to a May 26, 2022, article in *USA Today*.)

Scott is not the only female making waves in generosity. She is joined by others such as Laura Arnold. In the 2010s, the billionaire dedicated her life to fulltime philanthropy, signing The Giving Pledge and creating a private foundation focusing on education, health, tax policy, and criminal justice. "The Giving Pledge is a commitment by billionaires to voluntarily give most of their wealth to charitable causes either during their lifetimes or in their wills as bequests to be made after death," according to Hans Peter Schmitz writing for *The Conversation* in May 2022. In 2018, she took on the parole system with Jay-Z and Meek Mill by joining the REFORM Alliance board. Similarly, onetime reporter for *The Wall Street Journal* Cari Tuna cofounded Good Ventures with husband Dustin Moskovitz to oversee Open Philanthropy, a research and grantmaking foundation. And Priscilla Chan cofounded the Chan Zuckerberg Initiative to aid with grants and investments in science, education, social justice, and immigration.

Moreover, young people are getting into the action. Despite being hit with double financial whammies in the form of 2008's Great Recession and the 2020 pandemic, millennials give and in large numbers. "Nearly 3 out of 4 millennials (defined here as those ages 25 to 34) have sent some kind of financial aid to family or friends or donated to a nonprofit since the COVID-19 pandemic began, according to payment app Zelle's September (2020) Consumer Payment Behaviors report," writes Megan Leonhardt for CNBC. Even more astonishing? "That's the highest rate among any of the generations polled," according to the article.

So much for the young generation being unphilanthropic.

Myth 3: People Think Giving Is All About Money

"Charity" tends to conjure up associations of dollars and cents. Yes, monetary contributions play a huge role in generosity, but not the only one. More ways of giving abound. Tammy Day of the Civic Nebraska Writers Group tackled this subject in a piece on encouraging generosity in her state. "Communities can unleash their Nebraska generosity by redefining philanthropy as giving your time, talent, and treasure. This definition speaks to philanthropy's potential to shape communities' futures. It encompasses all parts of giving, includes all people in the process, and makes it an accessible part of civic life. Giving your time, talent, and treasure opens the door to giving and service, and invites everyone to come on in."

Day's distinction is essential for distinguishing between transactional (often characterized by one-off acts of kindness) and relational giving. Although both help, the latter can be seen as a long-term investment in a person, group, or community. For instance, rather than sending a check, a person might donate their time developing a bond with the recipient(s), producing lasting effects.

The list of ways to non-monetarily give are endless. Here are a few:

Volunteering

- **Habitat for Humanity:** Help build homes for those in need
- **Greenpeace:** Help protect our oceans and end the climate crisis
- **The CARE Project:** Help children and adults with hearing challenges

Tutoring/Mentoring

- **Youth Mentor:** Help at-risk youth out of the crime cycle in LA
- **Reading Partners:** Help students to read at grade level by fourth grade
- **Boys & Girls Club:** Help a young person with school, art, or sports

Product Donation

Eschewing money donations to aid others, organizations often donate items to assist the needy and disadvantaged. Examples include these:

- **Pharmaceutical companies:** Donating medication and medical supplies to support vulnerable populations
- **Restaurants:** Donating food to shelters and pantries
- **Optometrist groups:** Donating eyewear to the poor
- **Libraries:** Donating books to those lacking reading materials

Myth 4: Nonprofits Are Inefficient and Ineffective

In 2018, Felix Salmon wrote an article for *Slate* about "galanomics," a series examining the multibillionaire nonprofit sector.

> The mother of all galas took place on Monday: the annual Met Gala, which benefits The Metropolitan Museum of Art. Your own local gala will probably take place in a ballroom or some similarly grand space and will feature an abundance of circular tables for 10. You'll eat the kind of nondescript food designed to be served to hundreds of people simultaneously (hence the sobriquet "rubber chicken dinner"), sip cheap wine, and be subject to a cavalcade of speeches. The charity's executive director will talk, and so will the master of ceremonies (probably someone from television), as will a handful of honorees, employees, and other stakeholders. The reward for all this listening is . . . to watch the de rigueur slickly produced video. (If you're lucky, and you're very rich, and you're at an extremely high-end gala, you might be treated to a three-song set performed by Elton John or Jon Bon Jovi.)

The upshot of all this pomp and circumstance? A veritable windfall for the so-called gala economy, including caterers, event space holders, and society reporters. What about the charities themselves? Not so much. As Salmon relates, "I once saw a tiny nonprofit spend months organizing a blowout gala dinner, an endeavor which effectively became the full-time job of the entire staff. After all the costs were tallied from what seemed to be an extremely successful event, the gala ended up losing money for the organization."

This experience is not an isolated occurrence. In recent years, many have soured on nonprofits as wasteful and nonproductive. A fancy gala with attendees in their pearls and tuxes may be the most noxious example of conspicuous consumption masquerading as integrity, but it's no outlier. The public has come to distrust nonprofits and their activities due to the perception they're time wasters at best—and disingenuous money grabs at worst.

There are many causes for this viewpoint. For one, reports such as the 2022 Edelman Trust Barometer show that for the second straight year, nonprofits are perceived as less trustworthy than corporations. This is an unprecedented development; we will explore the reasons why it exists and persists in later chapters.

Ratings agencies also contribute to the problem. Charity Navigator and charity watchdogs are *supposed* to rate efficiency and effectiveness. Instead, to provide perceived value to their constituents, they engender cynicism. Rather than consider the actual progress groups are making, they tend to rate each nonprofit agency uniformly—even when they do quite different things. Worse, ever since *overhead* became a buzzword signaling malfeasance, nonprofits have struggled to not be labeled as wasteful, often to their detriment. Example: Many nonprofits fear investing in innovation to keep operating costs down.

But as Elijah Goldberg reported for *The Chronicle of Philanthropy* in August 2021, "Most nonprofits are highly effective. Check the data."

Goldberg points to examples of successes that go unreported. After all, with approximately 1.8 million nonprofit organizations in the US, the sector is filled with many mission-driven organizations that deliver goods and services with efficiency unparalleled in government and private sector companies.

Consider The Farmlink Project. Committed to solving "the problems of hunger and food waste," it was launched by a passionate group of college students in April 2020. Eager to do something to combat food inequality, it has rescued 75 million pounds of surplus food and delivered 62.5 million meals to those in need as of this writing. (More on this group in later chapters.) Likewise, international Charity: Water uses 100% of donations it acquires to provide water in developing nations. Since its founding in 2006, the group has given 15.4 million people around the world access to clean water by funding nearly 111,000 projects in 29 countries.

Myth 5: Philanthropy Is Broken

Let's be honest. People don't get into nonprofit work because they have tepid feelings about fixing things. No, the folks who choose to be involved are diehard enthusiasts hellbent on righting wrongs, improving the human condition, and making our world a better place to live for future generations. They tackle the most formidable challenges of our times.

Here is but a small sampling:

- Eradicating poverty
- Curing cancer
- Solving climate change
- Ending hunger

- Stopping human and animal trafficking
- Providing housing
- Improving literacy rates

Achieving success in any one of these causes is no walk in the park.

None of these problems are easy to solve. If they were, someone or some group would have done so by now. Instead, they are daunting challenges requiring Herculean efforts, complex organizational structures, buy-in from disparate decision-makers, supreme patience, and, of course, indefatigable grit.

The fact that mind-boggling problems still exist in the 21st century shouldn't be an indictment of nonprofits, their mission, their people, or their works. Most, if not all, societal issues pertinent to nonprofits can't easily be solved. Unfortunately, many well-meaning individuals and organizations have been unfairly criticized, even vilified by the public. Many factors account for this misperception, including scandals, reports of inefficiencies, and trust-eroding betrayals that unfairly malign organizations, if not the whole industry.

The truth is, we mustn't throw out the baby with the bathwater. Deficiencies and problems exist in the nonprofit realm. But they're also evident in the corporate sector. Generosity *does* work. And those committed to a better planet and a better way of life provide us so much in ways that often go unnoticed. We have the lives we do because of those who give—and those who enable such beneficence through their steadfast efforts. But if we are not vigilant, the many benefits we consider so essential to our lives will go away. In a similar fashion to how former Vice President Al

Gore's book (and later documentary) *An Inconvenient Truth* awakened the public to climate change in 2006—a crisis once below most people's radar—it's our hope that the book you're reading opens your eyes to the dangers of disappearing philanthropy. Before it's too late.

Now that we understand our crisis better, let's learn *why* it's happening.

CHAPTER 2

Why Our Crisis Exists

A young man named Tony walks into the cramped apartment he shares with his wife, Carmen, a scowl marring his face. His wife of two years looks up with sudden concern. She's used to seeing him exhausted at the end of another day juggling multiple gig economy jobs while looking for a full-time position in his chosen field. Yet today he looks more unhinged than usual. Putting her hand on his shoulder, she asks, "Baby, what's wrong?"

It takes a full second for Tony to check his emotions. "You know, I remember how my dad would get angry when he'd check the mail and get a handful of bills . . ."

"Yeah?" Carmen leads him over to the table so he can sit down.

"Back then I swore to myself, I'd never be like him. Now here I am, just 24 years old, and I've already turned into the guy." He waves the mail in front of his wife before continuing. "In addition to all these bills we've just received, our wonderful alma mater just sent me *another* donation request."

"They did?"

"Yeah. It's supposed to fund some new business school building. Um, last time I checked, they have $10 billion in the bank, and we have nothing.

Carmen snorts. "Um. Actually, it's worse than that. They sent two requests. One for each of us . . . and neither of us studied business!"

*****

A little backstory of Tony and Carmen is in order. Both Gen Zers graduated from a pricey California university. Each came from middle-class families that scrimped and saved so they could afford the hefty tuitions. It still wasn't enough. In addition to taking a private loan, Tony funded part of his engineering degree with tips he earned delivering pizzas to frat houses full of drunken classmates. For her part, Carmen tapped into a small inheritance she received on the death of her grandfather. Meant to cover her first home down payment, she took the money early to help her get a job. Unfortunately, her employment prospects remain dim even now. A graphic designer by trade, she earns inconsistent income via work for hire apps like Upwork and Fiverr.

Truth be told, Tony and Carmen consider each other to be the only decent things that came out of their college experience. This speaks to a key theme we will soon discuss. For now, let's tease it by stating the problem: Their alma mater not only doesn't know these two met and fell in love on campus—it is clueless about the deep connection Tony and Carmen have for their college—or *could* have had, harming its fundraising chances.

These days, Tony finds himself unable to secure a job in his field, placing much of the blame on the university he feels failed to prepare him for the real world. Carmen feels equally stymied, bitter at how her (quite expensive) education did little to improve her earning prospects. In fact, she often wishes she never attended at all, and instead invested her inheritance. Even during their university days, Tony and Carmen felt disengaged from the college they attended. Never a sports fan, Tony didn't bother to watch the school's teams, and Carmen spent little time on campus since she couldn't afford the dorms and had to commute. Not long ago, she deleted an email from a former classmate planning a reunion at the student union to mark their fourth year out in the "real world."

It must have been blatantly obvious to all that the young couple did not feel connected to their alma mater. Well, almost everyone. The only clueless party? The very entity whose engagement mattered most: the *university itself*.

Oblivious, their college nonetheless sends out donation appeals to Tony and Carmen every year like clockwork to support programs that neither benefited from. Also, the fact that two letters arrived on the same day—perfectly identical except for the names—is more galling, leading to Tony's outburst today and Carmen's similar disaffected feelings.

It's a good bet our university will *never* receive a gift from this couple even after they become more established. Why not? It employs a woefully disengaged and non-personalized approach to alumni relations. (It also doesn't help that Tony and Carmen feel like their tuition money was wasted. But that's another story.) Yes, this story is fictional, but it represents the reality for many college graduates, no matter their age or the college they attended.

In fact, something similar happened to one of the authors of this book.

"OH, YOU WANT YOUR DIPLOMA?"

Unlike our fictional characters Tony and Carmen, coauthor Michael does acknowledge the University of Missouri, commonly known as Mizzou, for setting him on the right path for professional success. Even so, Michael's reaction to alumni donation requests is not far off from Tony's indignation. Or Carmen's.

The negativity he feels toward his alma mater has little to do with the quality of his education and everything to do with how the university treated him. And his fellow classmates.

As a sophomore, Michael lived miles off campus in a house with friends. Like them, every day he'd drive to campus for class and fight the other students and faculty for the university's miniscule amount of parking. On many occasions, he'd end up with a ticket due to returning mere minutes after a meter expired—a rite of passage for many commuters. His roommate once complained to Michael, "One of the bathrooms in the business building has been closed for maintenance for three weeks, but if you miss the meter by 30 seconds you get a ticket. Maybe they should turn the meter readers into plumbers!"

The point is, Michael's wasn't a special case outlier. The university's extreme lack of parking, combined with eagle-eyed ticket jockeys, resulted in many students having massive citations to their name. For some, like Michael, these tickets mattered *after* they graduated, when Mizzou sprung its final red tape hassle.

As graduation drew near, Michael felt like he had achieved a monumental accomplishment. He was finally completing college after seemingly endless classes, study sessions in the library, and working two jobs his senior year. There was just one problem. Instead of a diploma, he received a notice asking him to show up at the admin building.

Upon entering, a bored-looking clerk confronted him. "What are you here for?"

With concern straining his voice, Michael said, "Well, I've just graduated, but I got this paper instead of my diploma. . . ."

The clerk looked at him and said the words he still hears in his head each time Mizzou solicits a donation: "Oh, you want your diploma? Well, you're not getting it until you pay off all these parking tickets we have on file."

Michael was stunned.

All that hard work, and all that *money*, and his university would hold up his diploma for some lousy outstanding parking tickets? Michael wrote a check from his skimpy savings to finally receive proof of his hard work. The net result? Mizzou gained a trifling amount of money for parking violations—but lost the lifelong support of a fresh grad who might have donated. For decades.

What Can Nonprofits Learn from These Stories

Universities, along with practically every other nonprofit, rely on a population of deeply invested people, such as alumni, to provide gifts, serving as the lifeblood of any organization. On average (all universities and colleges) alumni giving is equal to 23.2%, according to a piece on Ruffaloni.com titled "Higher Education Received $52.9B in Gifts in FY21: Alumni Lead Growth but Fewer Are Giving."

The chapter-opening story speaks directly to our Generosity Crisis. As our dramatization reveals, too many groups fail to invest their time developing significant connections that could literally pay dividends. Instead, they appear to be satisfied with limiting their interactions to the most superficial level: the transactional. For example: sending Tony and Carmen boilerplate letters relegates them to faceless pocketbooks for donation mining. Such organizations fail spectacularly to develop and build a deeper, more personal relationship. We call such efforts Radical Connection, which you'll learn more about throughout this book.

For now, it's imperative to recognize many nonprofits lack a deeper understanding of their communities. This problem would be bad enough for charitable giving on its own, but it's been exacerbated by a series of external and internal factors that have generated tremendous headwinds for nonprofits seeking to further their critical missions with the help of a charitable public.

First, let's consider the external problem. According to Arthur Brooks's *Who Really Cares; America's Charity Divide—Who Gives, Who Doesn't, and Why It Matters*, generosity was alive and well in 2006, the year before the book published. As Brooks writes, "There are far more charitable Americans than uncharitable ones. A large majority of U.S. citizens give money away: Approximately three out of four families make charitable donations each year. The average amount given by these families is $1800 or about 3.5% of household income."

Unfortunately for humanity, the figure quoted by Brooks in 2006—that three out of four, or roughly 75% of US households, give to charity—hasn't held true. In 2020, data from Giving USA, in partnership with the Lily Family School of Philanthropy at Indiana University, shows the number of Americans making charitable gifts has reached an all-time low. As we shared in the Introduction, for the first time ever, the percentage of Americans who donate in any way has dipped below 50%, which means the percentages of Americans giving to charity annually is sure to decline into the single digits within just a short 49 years.

Also, according to a longitudinal study by Gallup, which has studied giving and volunteerism annually since 2000, the United

States has witnessed a 16% decline in the number of Americans who give, just since the turn of this century. Even more conservative efforts measured by a Giving USA study demonstrate that the percentage of those who make gifts to charitable organizations has decreased by 13% in the same period. The United States is not alone in this decline, as Canada is following a similar fate with a 6.1% decline of the percentage of individuals who give to charitable causes, down from 25% in 2000 to 19.4% in 2018. That decrease is a scary thought. It's a preview of the decades to come if we don't revolutionize the business of generosity. Before addressing the major challenge of establishing Radical Connection, the solution to our Generosity Crisis, let's examine the causes for generosity's degradation.

EXTERNAL FACTORS

The following sections describe the outside reasons leading to philanthropy's decline.

It's the IRS, Silly

"In this world, nothing is certain except death and taxes." Benjamin Franklin's famous quote makes us wonder if the late statesman had a time machine allowing him to witness the Internal Revenue Service (IRS) in its modern iteration. Recent tax code changes have negatively affected charitable gift giving. To understand how, context is required. But first, let us say we recognize taxes are a hot-button issue. It's not our intention to argue higher taxes are good or regular Americans should be punished or even considered in a negative light due to how tax changes affect their giving behaviors.

Instead, let's look at the facts. Under the previous administration, the tax code changed considerably for most Americans in 2018. Some of these shifts resulted in lower taxes for many citizens, but that still didn't translate into greater giving. In fact, lower- and middle-income earners were *disincentivized* from philanthropy. This is because if their giving was driven in the past from getting a tax break, IRS changes, such as a higher standard deduction, removed their primary motivation.

Pam Norley, president of Fidelity Charitable, a charitable-giving vehicle managing donations for people and organizations, explains: "An incentive to give will definitely increase giving, no question about that. For many, it may not be a matter of whether to give, it's how much to give. If I know I'll get a tax deduction, then, yeah, there's a capability of giving more." GUSA also tracked a decline of individual giving in 2018 of 1.1%.

To be sure, these tax changes obviously had an impact. But what were the changes and how did they hurt donations to nonprofits?

Increased Standard Deduction

The tax code change sending the greatest shockwaves throughout the nonprofit economy in 2018 came from the increase in the standard deduction available to taxpayers. It roughly doubled, severely hampering charitable giving for those who primarily viewed their gifts as an opportunity to pay less money to Uncle Sam every April. The logic works like this: If taxpayers use charitable giving to increase itemized deductions, then lose the incentive to pursue itemized deductions, charitable giving will drop. To turn Norley's quote on its head, "If I know I'm not itemizing my deductions, then, yeah, there's not a capability of giving more."

In a related follow-up, CNBC reported 16.7 million tax returns claimed itemized deductions after the change, down from 46.2 million in 2017. The takeaway? Most lower- and middle-earning taxpayers lost interest in itemizing deductions.

Increased Estate and Gift Tax Exclusion

The Tax Act of 2018 seemed to be fixated on doubling things. Besides the standard deduction, the tax code changes also doubled the estate and gift tax exclusion amount and generation-skipping tax exemption. This increased to a whopping $11.18 million. Such a massive increase removed the incentive for Americans to plan charitable donations on one's death to avoid estate taxes.

Reduction of the Top Income Tax Bracket

The tax rates changed greatly for many brackets in 2018. Of note is the difference to top earners. The highest tax rate as of 2020 for single taxpayers making more than $500,000 or married couples earning more than $600,000, was set at 37%, a decline from 2017's rate of 39.6%. These taxpayers, who certainly do use itemized deductions, had less enticement to donate for deductions' sake as their overall tax bill fell.

Cutting Out Other Itemized Deductions

The 2018 tax changes also affected several popular deductions, including state and local tax payments, a change today's administration is fighting against and trying to restore. At first glance, a reduction of available deductions may lead you to assume taxpayers would use charitable gifts to shore up the difference, but in practice, when combined with the doubling of the standard deduction and the doubling of the estate tax exemption, it induces more taxpayers to lean toward the standard deduction.

The Death of the 80/20 Rule

This one hit fans of college sports right in the gut. The 2018 tax changes repealed the 80/20 rule, allowing taxpayers to deduct 80% of any amounts paid to an educational nonprofit for the right to buy tickets to sporting events. For football fans who enjoyed the game more knowing they were generating a tax deduction, it was like a fourth-quarter interception by the opposing team.

TAX CHANGES MADE GIVING TRICKIER

The 2018 tax changes weren't *all* negative from a donation perspective. There are some alternative vehicles still available for giving, but they tend to be more technical than the straightforward itemized deductions so many are used to, leading to the giving bottlenecks we will discuss at the end of this section.

IRA-Qualified Charitable Distribution

The IRA Qualified Charitable Distribution (QCD) rule allows holders of IRA accounts possessing pretax money to donate untaxed funds to a nonprofit of their choice on a tax-free basis. This is especially important for taxpayers over the age of 72 because they are required to take the minimum withdrawal. If the money isn't needed yet, the QCD rule remains a perfect choice.

Bunching

Finally, a tax term that's exactly what it sounds like! Bunching is the strategy of taking donations planned over several years and collecting them into one larger sum made in a single year. Bunching donations may create a total amount larger than the standard deduction, making the itemized deduction for the charitable donation an attractive option.

Donor-Advised Funds

Donor-advised funds (DAFs) share certain traits and tax advantages with charitable trusts and private foundations but are much quicker and cheaper to set up. They also come with the significant side benefit of public anonymity. This enables a donor to give without disclosing their motivations directly to a nonprofit organization. Think of them as a good option for a high-net-worth individual whose wealth isn't large enough to make a trust or foundation a no-brainer. (Note: These are also sometimes referred to as philanthropic checking accounts.)

Notably, DAFs have exploded in the past 20 years, making Fidelity Charitable "technically" the largest nonprofit in the country. According to the National Philanthropic Trust's 2021 Donor Advised Fund Report, charitable assets under management in all DAFs totaled $159.83 billion in 2020, a 9.9% increase from the revised 2019 total of $145.49 billion. In addition, DAF contributions in 2020 totaled $47.85 billion. This represents a 20.6% increase over the revised 2019 value of $39.69 billion. What's more, the number of individual DAF accounts in the US rose by 16.3% to 1,005,099, passing the 1 million mark for the first time.

Avoiding Realized Capital Gains via Giving

An individual holding appreciated property such as mutual funds or common stock that has increased in value can donate this property directly to a charity instead of selling and then cutting a check. This avoids the need to report capital gains on the sale of the property or investment as long as it's held for at least one year.

WHY THIS MATTERS—OR TWO PROBLEMS FOR THE PRICE OF ONE

This may sound convoluted for someone lacking a tax background so we will simplify the problem. The real issue is that tax code changes complicate the donation process for many good-willed citizens. Just as paralysis by analysis can thwart a salesperson's attempt to close a deal, so can a complex tax system hinder the average American's giving inclination. Put simply: Tax complexity adds friction to the giving process, reducing generosity.

However, high-net-worth individuals aren't particularly concerned about changes to the tax code. Multimillionaires and billionaires don't need the tax write-off, so they essentially ignore this aspect of the interplay between taxes and charitable gifting. But as the shift from itemized deductions to standard deductions shows, we nonetheless face a large-scale problem thanks to these changes. Millions on millions of taxpayers in this country have modified or will modify their giving based on IRS changes.

This is problem one. The second problem exposed by tax changes is the delicate balancing act between giving motivations. Some donors contribute out of the goodness of their hearts. Others act for more pragmatic reasons. In reality, most who give to charitable causes and nonprofits do so based on a combination of these factors. To this point, coauthor Brian Crimmins recalls attending a nonprofit board meeting at which a colleague matter-of-factly announced, "I'm happy to give my time to help this group, but once the standard deduction wipes out my tax write-off, I just can't keep giving financially. There's nothing in it for me."

This is a micro example of a macro problem: keeping a healthy balance of rationales for giving (even) when external factors throw things out of whack.

MORE ON DONOR FRICTION

As discussed, friction slows things down and, in some cases, can effectively stop a benevolent intention in its tracks. In its least damaging form, it creates inefficiencies. For decades, Silicon Valley wisely put its best minds on removing friction from the sales process. It's now astoundingly easy for customers to make a purchase on Amazon. (Ask anyone who has ever had a small child or pet place one.) Tax changes, however, introduce more friction to the world of philanthropy in the form of confusion. If people must stop and think, or figure out new rules, they are less likely to give. Amazon and other for-profit companies have made things so easy, so personalized, that Americans have come to expect such ease. Accordingly, they tend to balk at giving when non-profits can't keep up.

Here's one more way to think about this. Consider the average taxpayer. They may be familiar with tax-advantaged areas of the law, whether it's their 401(k) from work or how giving to a 501(c)(3) will be deductible at tax time. Now go back to that average taxpayer and try explaining the benefits of *bunching*, a term they've likely never heard before, at least in relation to taxes. You'll see them lose interest in supporting your mission almost immediately.

THE CROWDING OUT EFFECT

According to *Investopedia*, this phenomenon occurs when an increase in public sector spending reduces or even eliminates private sector expenditures. In recent years, a new spin on this old problem comes from the rise of so-called philanthrocapitalism. Nowadays, more companies claiming a virtuous mission are gifting, giving, and donating. So are private rich donors.

The media loves these types of feel-good stories and tend to lavish them not just with praise, but also with heavy coverage. *What's wrong with that?* You might ask. Simple. Such conspicuous contributions disincline the public to give. When high-profile donors such as MacKenzie Scott gift millions and millions of dollars to a charity, it has a big impact on the average person. As we shall discuss throughout this book, giving is largely an *emotional* activity.

Scott's acts of extravagant selfless generosity, along with those of her peers, can have unforeseen and deleterious consequences. Everyday people are likely to feel like their check for $100 to the same organization is pointless. More alarmingly, this has resulted in the wealthy comprising a larger percentage of total giving. Anecdotally, coauthor Nathan provided pro bono consulting for a nonprofit that received a Scott gift not long ago. They were concerned about announcing the windfall out of concern that other loyal community patrons might stop giving should the information be made public. They called Nathan for advice as to whether they should announce the donation or not. Ultimately, they held a small private event for their board and key stakeholders to share the news but decided not to do any media blasts.

COMPETITION BETWEEN NONPROFITS

According to the Independent Sector, a national coalition of nonprofits, foundations, and corporate-giving programs, there are currently 1.8 million nonprofits in America today, each with their own budgets and needs. On any given day, a person might be solicited by several different organizations, some they may have heard of, others they haven't. We certainly aren't stating there are too many nonprofits, but at such a pronounced scale, philanthropy invariably devolves into a competition for hearts and wallets. So many organizations vying daily for attention and gifts is problematic. Even well-meaning individuals keen on doing good are bound to feel overwhelmed by the choices. This speaks to the friction problem.

PROLIFERATION OF OMNI-CHANNEL MESSAGING

Of course, all these charities aren't just sending out simple mailers to the homes of people like Tony and Carmen. The rise of omni-channel fundraising strategies means the typical donor simply can't get away from solicitations. They come in a plethora of forms beyond traditional mail: phone calls, text messages, social media DMs, email, expensive mail premiums with return address labels, pens, or branded tote bags. Also, SEO wizards and Google Ad impresarios are constantly developing novel ways to ensure your search results lead you to ever more convenient ways to give.

Although we applaud such digital ingenuity, the unintended consequence of the status quo is that people with limited attention spans, not to mention limited bandwidths, have an ever-diminishing ability to discern organizational credibility. They're also so deluged with messaging they're apt not to research if a given organization's mission resonates with them. (We will explore this topic in more detail as it relates to overall distrust in Chapter 6.)

SHIFTING VALUES TOWARD ALTRUISM

Especially on the East Coast, wealthy families have traditionally aligned themselves with a specific cause they support genera-tionally. But the legacy of handing down a family mission to each generation is rapidly changing. Coauthor Nathan once worked with a billionaire who gave hundreds of millions of dollars to a charity his family long supported. However, he did not pass that custom down to his own children. "They should find their own path. Discover their own causes," he told Nathan.

In his mind, this wealthy individual meant to foster a sense of independence in his progeny. Perhaps it worked and his offspring found their own pet causes. But what if it didn't? With so many older people emulating this man's actions, the resulting independence is sure to erode the core societal values once underpinning America.

This change in attitude isn't limited to the children of the ultra-wealthy. The millennial generation is seeking new ways to be charitable—separating the size of the check from passion for a cause. Many prefer to donate time and energy to causes, as evidenced by the popularity of sites like HelpStay, connecting youth with volunteering opportunities around the world.

LOSING OUR RELIGION

According to a 2021 GUSA report, religion is the driving force behind the largest share (27%) of the $484.85 billion donated by Americans yearly. This phenomenon can't help but create a problem as fewer Americans report being spiritual than any time in the past. According to Pew Research, from 2007 to 2018, the percentage of Americans who claim no religious affiliation rose from 16% to 26%, a considerable leap in just one decade. As you might expect, giving to religious organizations fell by 3.9% in 2018 when adjusted for inflation.

HAPPINESS IS TRENDING NEGATIVE

A study published in *Nature Communications* by researchers from the University of Zurich showed a clear connection between generosity and happiness. Experiments, including MRI brain scans, show that even the *promise* to donate can increase happiness levels. That sounds like great news for nonprofits, right? The bad news is worldwide happiness has been trending down in recent decades. In fact, the World Happiness Report, measuring happiness since 1973, has found self-reported levels have plunged since the early 1990s. Worse, Gallup's Global Emotions 2020 poll held the percentage of respondents who reported smiling or laughing in the past 24 hours had plunged to a *record low*.

SUSPICION TOWARD INSTITUTIONS

According to the United Nations, the percentage of Americans who trust the government has slid from 73% in 1958 to just 24% in 2021. Western Europe has suffered a similar decline since the 1970s, although not as dramatic. Interestingly, this deterioration isn't purely a generational issue. Millennials and boomers alike show a similar level of distrust for the government and other institutions buttressing society. Collapsing confidence matters to the nonprofit community especially because doubt toward one entity tends to spread to others. Also, if a person doesn't trust the government, why would they trust a university, an international charity, even a local philanthropic cause? We saw this phenomenon with Tony and Carmen.

*****

The external issues discussed in this chapter are critical to fathoming the Generosity Crisis, but please do not be fooled into thinking this overview sufficiently explains the causes or the challenge of fostering needed awareness. Returning to the problem and going off gross revenue, 2021 would appear to be another banner year for philanthropy. In reality, it exposed dangerous cracks to our giving model. When adjusted for inflation, giving decreased by 0.7%.

Just as troubling, many people believe we are in the "golden age of giving." Nothing could be further from the truth. As mentioned, if not for a single megadonor like Scott propping up annual donation totals, total giving in 2021 would have slid even further. Consider this: Mega gifts, as defined by Giving USA in 2020, are gifts of $350 million or more. In 2020, Giving USA categorized $10.1 billion in donations as mega gifts, compared with $14.9 billion in 2021. During this same period, the increase in the number of billionaires increased by 107 between 2020 (2,668) and 2021 (2,755). In 2021, total giving as a percentage of GDP decreased (from 2.3% in 2020 to 2.1% in 2021), but nearly $5 billion more in gifts were attributed as mega gifts.

We conclude that ultra-high-net-worth (UHNW) individuals continued to play an increasingly larger role in 2021. Mathematically speaking, $4.8 billion less was contributed by non-UHNW individuals. With an average gift of $813 for non-UHNW individuals, this equates to more than 5.9 million fewer charitable gift transactions given by individuals in 2021 alone. A simple glimpse beneath the hood reveals the core problem: The percentage of Americans giving money is decreasing. And it will continue to free-fall for one big reason: Philanthropy is not about money. It is about relationships—and the baseline relationships between nonprofits and their donors is eroding. That's why understanding the *internal causes* driving this problem is of such critical importance.

Billionaires can't prop up philanthropy forever.

INTERNAL FACTORS

The following sections describe individual causes leading to philanthropy's decline.

Lack of Innovation Investment

Organizations such as charity watchdogs evaluate nonprofits based on their efficiency, examining what percentage of donations are applied to an organization's core mission. Unfortunately, the zeal to keep efficiency high means investments in innovation are kept low, limiting nonprofits' ability to keep up with consumer expectations.

Entrepreneur, author, and humanitarian activist Dan Pallotta discussed this challenge in a 2013 TED Talk, demarcating the difference in what we expect from the private sector and charities. As Pallotta explained, "[Unlike corporations] nonprofits are not allowed to try new things. It makes us think that overhead is a negative, that it is somehow not a part of 'the cause.' This forces organizations to forego what they need for growth."

TAKING DONORS FOR GRANTED

Coauthor Nathan clearly remembers the worst thing he ever heard from a donor: "Why is it that I only hear from your organization when you want more money?" Nathan knew in that moment that the donor felt their interactions were purely transactional instead of based on a strong relationship. This is no outlier anecdote. Too often, the business practices and success metrics of nonprofits encourage such transactional thinking. If an annual fundraising goal is the primary measurement of one's actions and the number of donors kept year-over-year is not considered as important, of course the importance of building life-long relationships with donors will fall by the wayside.

To their credit, nonprofit leaders almost uniformly recognize that a transactional approach to donors is not in the best long-term interest of either their organization or their donors.

And yet for a variety of reasons, often related to short-term funding gaps, they continue to set targets yearly that encourage thinking about quotas to hit instead of relationships to build. In essence, they've created a leaky bucket that can never be filled.

FAILURE TO STAY TRUE TO THE MISSION

Ultimately, the real purpose of most nonprofits is to put themselves out of business. Think about charities dedicated to eradicating diseases such as cancer. Or ending poverty. If the organization achieves its goals, there is no longer a need for the nonprofit. But sometimes organizations will stray from their core mission, whether they have achieved their goal not.

This leads to distrust from a public that is inclined to question the motives of a charity that's forever asking for more money, even after the stated mission is achieved. Conversely, one positive example of this is City of Hope. Once founded as a tuberculosis sanitarium, it reinvented itself as a cancer hospital after eliminating the threat of TB. Reborn as a world-renowned cancer center, its new goal, as it should be for every nonprofit, is to put itself out of business by fulfilling its intended purpose.

FAILURE TO ENGAGE IN A MEANINGFUL WAY

Nonprofits lacking transparency and relationship capital often don't connect with donors because the latter don't know where their money is going. Too many organizations lack a sense of intimacy and trust with their communities. Prospective donors with little faith in these organizations' activities, and doubts about their integrity, are prone to question their raison d'etre as well as whether to donate to them. On the other end of the spectrum, if the measure of a nonprofit's success is its relationships, not money, fundraising ceases to be a barrier to engagement.

Instead, it becomes one more tool to increase the focus and alignment between an organization and its supporters.

TECHNOLOGY REINFORCING TRANSACTIONAL VERSUS TRANSFORMATIONAL GIVING

Innovation can be used for good or evil, and often the difference is extremely subtle. Sometimes, cutting-edge tools are seized on by nonprofits with the promise of raising big money. But what happens when this is done in a surface-level, *transactional* way? It erodes affiliations, squandering opportunities for what we term Radical Connection. One example: In the race to adopt AI tools for prospecting, some organizations trade long-term relationships for short-term dollars, never a recipe for success.

Coauthor Nathan witnessed firsthand how tech and business practices can encourage transactional relationships. He once consulted with a successful organization, interviewing different teams as part of his work. In doing so, he discovered the administrator overseeing the direct mail campaigns had never even met with the major gift team during his 10 years on the job. The administrator had achieved some of his goals based on his correspondence yet failed to seize the opportunity to encourage stronger relationships with so many important supporters. Unwittingly, the organization was encouraging major donors to give the same amount yearly instead of becoming more deeply involved in the cause.

FAILURE TO IDENTIFY THE RIGHT PEOPLE AT THE RIGHT TIME FOR THE RIGHT PURPOSE

Sadly, legacy fundraising practices are based on the erroneous idea *every* person in your community can be a potential donor.

Highly inefficient as a strategy, this can result in tremendous waste of money and time. Example: If only 49% of Americans give to nonprofits, why on earth would an organization approach everyone and hope for the best?

Another name for this approach, still employed by many organizations to this day, is "spray and pray." Spray-and-pray fundraising rarely helps organizations meet their goals in meaningful ways. As marketing experts are quick to point out, this tactic fails for three reasons. First, a cause may be irrelevant to the masses. Also, to people bombarded with messages daily, a spray-and-pray fundraising message won't make the cut. Second, such solicitations are interruptive—a prospect annoyed by a message is no longer a potential donor. Third, and most seriously, these appeals are unengaging. Transactional messaging is the enemy of deep connection, and the shotgun approach is transactional by definition.

INCORRECTLY PIGEONHOLING PEOPLE AS FIXED DONORS OR NON-DONORS

Many organizations still operate under the incorrect hypothesis their community can be quickly sorted into two roles: that of donor or non-donor. Defining people in binary terms fails to account for the fact every member of the community is an individual who can dynamically move closer to (or further away from) a group. Therefore, creating this designation and leaving community members in stasis leads to more transactional fundraising, the opposite of how for-profits treats their customers.

Instead, nonprofits should learn from how companies in the general economy disrupted their approach to the public. The most successful now employ a decided shift toward *personalization* to improve customer service and loyalty. If companies can recognize people are individual humans and not merely consumers, nonprofits can do the same thing with donors. When an organization discovers their donors' passions, desires, and concerns, they are building a deeper relationship than they could ever dream of. They are engaging in Radical Connection.

FAILURE TO DISCERN AND MEASURE GENEROSITY'S REAL MOTIVATORS

Nonprofits tend to theorize about what their perfect donor looks like based on incomplete data such as a limited time frame or the tepid results of a spray-and-pray campaign. The result is an overly simplified and often biased model that attempts to provide simple answers for complex and often emotional decisions donors make yearly.

But as classical fundraising training will reinforce, there are three big elements that must be sufficiently addressed for people to give money to nonprofits: emotional, financial, rational. (In this book, we will return again and again to the emotional because we believe it to be the most powerful of the three.) Not surprisingly, each of these elements may have hundreds of variables contributing to a final decision. Figuring all of this out is such a colossal task that many organizations still go straight to wealth data to identify rich prospects, regardless of whether those individuals may be part of the 51% of Americans who don't make charitable gifts. This legacy approach is not a winning strategy and only reinforces so many of the negative stereotypes and biases that got us into the Generosity Crisis in the first place.

CORPORATE AMERICA HAS YOUR NUMBER

One of the greatest shifts in the modern economy is corporate America's ability to connect with consumers on a *values level.*

(Once more, this speaks to the emotional aspect we wish to emphasize.) Look around to see this in action. Seemingly every product on the grocery store shelf has a values statement associated with it these days: organic, cruelty-free, made in America, and so on.

Connecting with consumers in this mission-based way is not only profitable for companies but also a threat to society's giving behaviors. In effect, it's undermining the public's willingness to give. Undoubtedly, the reigning champion of values marketing is Elon Musk. Musk once described his various companies by saying: "SpaceX, Tesla, Neuralink, and The Boring Company are philanthropy. If you say philanthropy is love of humanity, they are philanthropy. Tesla is accelerating sustainable energy. This is a love of philanthropy."

Clearly, Musk is no fool, the kind of business leader who would dare send some boilerplate message of the variety Tony and Carmen received. Rather, he's been so successful in his messaging by tapping into the *emotional* component of people's decision-making. This can't help but suggest huge implications for generosity. In our next chapter, we'll examine how corporations are getting this right—okay, they're *killing it*—while nonprofits continue to flail.

CHAPTER 3

From Shareholder Value to Shareholder Values

Jamal merges onto Pacific Coast Highway with giddy anticipation. It's his first time out in his brand-new Tesla Model X, a top-of-the-line model featuring three motors. Now he wants to really open it up on this iconic highway. After all, the Tesla salesperson wowed Jamal with impressive stats: zero to 60 in just 2.5 seconds, a quarter-mile time of under 10 seconds, and more than 1,000 horsepower with an extremely high torque unique to electric motors. Pressed back into his leather seat, Jamal floors it. He notices admiring glances from other drivers as he nimbly zips in and out of traffic. Looking down, he marvels at all the digital features. *It's like an iPhone on wheels.*

But our newly minted Tesla owner isn't only thrilled by his new car's performance. He's joyful knowing he's doing his part to save the world.

All this horsepower and comfort comes sans environmental harm. In his head, he tallies all the gas he *won't* be burning up flying down the PCH. However, he doesn't spare a thought for the fact he's cruising on top of a 1,300-pound battery composed of exotic metals mined in brutal places like the Congo, or that the electricity to recharge his car will likely come from a coal- or gas-fired power plant. Neither of those facts appear in Tesla's expert marketing and sales campaign—only the good he'll be doing for the earth, plus the fun he'll have accomplishing it.

Zooming down the California coast, Jamal passes a billboard for the Sierra Club, an organization he's contributed to for the past 10 years. Even before making partner at his environmental law firm, Jamal felt contributing to charities was an integral part of his obligation to protect the planet. Pondering the sign as he whizzes past, Jamal figures he'll take a year off donating.

The $140,000 sticker price of his new car just put a major dent in his budget. He also rationalizes that the Sierra Club probably won't miss his donation.

After all, he hasn't exactly received any special communiqués from the group thanking him for his large (by his standards) donation lately, just a few generic form letters. "Dear Mr. Evans, we here at the Sierra Club appreciate your continued support . . ." He hasn't even been approached to volunteer his time or to speak to the organization about pressing legal issues. He wonders, "If my contribution is this shiny new Tesla, what's so wrong with that?"

For his part, Jamal supports other charities, for instance, protecting the oceans and safeguarding the ecosystem for future generations, though he's too busy to have his own kids yet. All these donations could be put on pause, Jamal thinks, due to two key factors: his whopping new monthly car payment, and the sense of fatigue he feels toward charities overall.

"It's like every day I get another mailer from some nonprofit I've never heard of begging me for more cash," he vented to a friend last week.

"You, too?" said Anne. "I get the same spammy notices 24/7. Yet none of them seem to know more about me other than my name and address."

"Right. And they expect us to shell out all this money without proving they'll ever use it as promised?"

Meanwhile, *everyone* Jamal and Anne know seems to accept that Tesla vehicles are the future of green-friendly travel. A constant media drumbeat portraying Elon Musk as the ideal environmental leader doesn't hurt, either. The more Jamal considers it, the clearer his thinking becomes. He's made his decision: Buying a Tesla was his last big gift to philanthropy this year.

INSIGHTS FROM JAMAL'S STORY

In Chapter 2 we documented a variety of external and internal factors plaguing nonprofits' fundraising efforts. These dynamics have snowballed, creating a vacuum of disengagement between charitable organizations and donors like Jamal. Aristotle famously postulated "nature abhors a vacuum." We might add capitalism despises it even more—and often rushes in to fill it. The result? Corporations are more in tune with consumers than ever before, using unprecedented intimacy to tug at the public's heart strings, creating a trust level that nonprofits always had, yet now struggle to maintain. This new relationship paradigm has altered how so many of us view giving. Consider Jamal's story. According to his logic, if he can do good by buying a Tesla *and* get a lightning-fast car that turns heads, it's a win-win. And Musk certainly is winning. As of this writing he is the world's richest man, on track to be the world's first trillionaire.

Our man Musk isn't alone in blurring the line between capitalism and philanthropy. He isn't even an early adopter of a new corporate style emphasizing mission-driven values. For decades, business management focused on increasing shareholder returns, often at the expense of employees and the environment. This pursuit often created a short-sighted mentality promoting quarterly profits over any other consideration. But things shifted in recent years. More and more companies adopted the logic of Salesforce.com co-CEO Marc Benioff, who said, "I think business is the greatest platform for change. The great miscalculation of the age is the idea that businesses have to make a choice: to become profitable or to become platforms for change."

Elon Musk's Tesla is one of many successful outfits pushing a message of philanthrocapitalism, but many other brands have perfected their approach over the years. Our message to nonprofits is this: Pay close attention to how the most successful companies with strong values now operate. Your effectiveness, messaging, and perhaps very existence depend on it. If you ever want to level up, you would do well to learn from these exemplars.

To assist, we've listed some compelling corporate examples in the coming sections.

PATAGONIA

Founded in 1973 by avid rock climber Yvon Chouinard, this company made and sold the types of top-shelf outdoor clothing and gear this sportsman might use himself. It's evolved from its founding as a smaller organization, yet its commitment to quality products never wavered. Patagonia's environmental devotion remains stronger than ever, even as it has grown into a billion-dollar enterprise. Unlike many competitors, Patagonia's mission statement has nothing to do with profit or maximizing shareholders' return on investment. It simply reads, "We're in business to save our home planet."

Equally as distinct, Patagonia possesses four core values:

- Build the best product.
- Cause no unnecessary harm.
- Use business to protect nature.
- Do not be bound by convention.

That last entry—do not be bound by convention—has been at the heart of how this company markets itself to its loyal customer base. Patagonia makes high-quality, high-priced clothing, and its following expects the best. Although devoted customers may line up to buy the latest offering, in 2013 Patagonia launched an unusual advertising campaign that trade publication *Marketing Week* called "part nudge, part shock tactic." Along with a picture of the apparel, the ad said in big bold letters, "DON'T BUY THIS JACKET."

How does telling potential customers *not* to purchase your products help your business? If anything, it should undermine it, right? Not exactly. For the brass at Patagonia, this message reinforced every one of its core values. It also communicated to its established base the jacket they buy yearly (or purchased five years ago) is just as good today as when they bought it. There's no need to replace it quite yet.

As the company's marketing director at the time Johnathan Perry explained, "We're at the opposite spectrum of big brand disposable fashion. We're about making great-quality products that are designed to last, so we have a lifetime warranty on our products." In short, there is no need to buy another Patagonia jacket anytime soon because the company isn't trying to swindle you into more purchases via planned obsolescence. Their stuff is made that well.

To be sure, Patagonia was expressing philanthrocapitalist ideas almost a decade before they were in vogue. Perry continued, "Our customers expect very high quality and that's why they always come back to us. At the same time, we help consumers change their behavior for the better by encouraging them to make more considered purchases."

BEN & JERRY'S

As well known for its social conscience as for its iconic ice cream pints, the company was started as a single Vermont parlor in 1978 by Ben Cohen and Jerry Greenfield, maturing into a national institution by the 1980s and a global brand shortly thereafter. The founders set themselves apart by being a "social justice company that makes ice cream." Their winning formula combines activism, creative marketing, and an emphasis on building brand loyalty. Ben & Jerry's operates under three missions at once: "to make fantastic ice cream," "to manage our company for sustainable growth," and "to make the world a better place." That last nugget is particularly important as the company is universally known for its social values and public statements.

Ben & Jerry's has three core values:

- Human rights and dignity

- Social and economic justice

- Environmental protection, restoration, and regeneration

CEO Matthew McCarthy was recently interviewed by the *Harvard Business Review* and explained how Ben & Jerry's is at the center of social issues. "We do these things not to sell more ice cream but because we care about people and have values. All businesses are collections of people with values; it's a force that's always there. But companies usually make their values known through things like lobbying: money that never sees the light of day. I believe that increasingly, in a world of hyper-transparency, if you're not making your values known publicly, you're putting your business and brand at risk." Such activism has paid off well, not just for society but the bottom line. It's been a boon for Ben & Jerry's business. McCarthy explains, "We're seeing strong growth, and we've got some good data showing that our fans are aware of our social mission activities, which makes them more supportive of our business and vocal about it. Some of them buy more ice cream as a result. They don't have to. That's why we call them fans, not consumers."

Now that's powerful branding. However, truth be told, the company's activism can also court serious controversy. In summer 2021, Ben & Jerry's announced it would no longer allow sales of its products in what's labeled "occupied Palestinian territory" in Israel. This controversial move caused backlash from both conservative and liberal politicians, Jewish activists, and Israel itself. Prime Minister Naftali Bennett called the boycott "anti-Israeli," and states including Florida and New York vowed to divest from parent company Unilever over what they considered to be participation in the boycott, divestment, and sanctions (BDS) movement.

As of this writing, Ben & Jerry's remains firm in its position.

THE BODY SHOP

The Body Shop's green stores are a ubiquitous part of most every shopping center in America, but the company emerged from humble beginnings. Anita Roddick founded it in 1976 with a single store in Brighton, England. Similar to Patagonia, The Body Shop leapt into existence because its founder had trouble finding products that not only met her high standards (for skin care) but also possessed high integrity. Roddick's vision centered on selling ethically sourced, cruelty-free products featuring natural ingredients. From the outset, none of The Body Shop's products were tested on animals. All were made with ingredients sourced directly from producers instead of relying on wholesalers and middle operators who might not share such devotion to quality and ethics. Purpose-based, the company's mission is to "fight for a fairer, more beautiful world."

It pursues this cause through three core beliefs:

- Business can be a force for good.
- Everyone is beautiful.
- Fight to empower women and girls.

In a 2006 interview with *The Guardian*, Roddick explained the hard work that goes into holding up the brand's reputation for ethics. "You need purchasing programs and to have a dialogue in the most honorable way with the most fragile and poorest communities you are working with. You have to ask them if you can purchase from them and under what conditions and how much you would have to pay as a social premium. This has always been the language of The Body Shop and this is the bit that makes me want to sing with joy."

Through the years, The Body Shop has advanced a legacy of moral business practices, refusing to sell products tested on animals, and advocating for women and girls despite being first acquired by L'Oréal and later Brazilian cosmetics company Natura. Just as Ben & Jerry's stayed true to its core values even after being attained by Unilever, being owned by giant companies did not derail The Body Shop. As Roddick explained at the time of the L'Oréal buyout, "I'm not an apologist for them, I'm just excited that I can be like a Trojan horse and go into that huge business and talk about how we can buy ingredients like cocoa butter from Ghana and sesame oil from Nicaraguan farmers and how we can do that in a kindly, joyful way, and that is happening."

KEY TAKEAWAYS FOR NONPROFITS

Just over 50 years ago, famed economist Milton Friedman stated, "There is one and only one social responsibility of business—to use its resources and engage in activities designed to increase its profits." Back when Patagonia, Ben & Jerry's, and The Body Shop began, their business model seemed crazy to many people. How they functioned appeared to be the opposite of traditional capitalism: putting values before profits. Yet, despite how the traditional business community once sneered at them, each triumphed. These companies were (and are) outliers blazing a new trail, one combining values with commerce. As a result, many corporations in diverse industries—including Tesla—have followed suit.

All three example companies started in the 1970s, an era of deep social upheaval, fertile ground for radical new ideas in commerce. Most important, they haven't compromised their values in the ensuing decades. Patagonia became a top global brand but has maintained its environmental commitment. Though acquired by corporate behemoth Unilever, Ben & Jerry's remains steadfast in its mission-centric values. The Body Shop has been purchased by two separate major corporations yet stays cruelty-free and ethically sourced.

Facing down their own set of external and internal challenges, these companies navigated them more skillfully than many nonprofits. They proved the naysayers wrong, demonstrating how a business could enjoy profits and growth without sacrificing ethics and/or core beliefs. In fact, as Ben & Jerry's McCarthy explained, its values and activism became a *profits driver*, increasing brand loyalty. The same holds true for the other two companies. Their successes are admired as models, showing consumers buying products and services needn't be an either/or proposition between getting a good deal and ethical values. The ensuing major insight can be boiled down to this: "You don't have to choose between 'good for me' or 'good for the world,' you can have it both ways—and at the same time."

The net result from all three examples is any businessperson's dream. Patagonia, Ben & Jerry's, and The Body Shop remain market leaders in their industries, with strong balance sheets and devoted consumers (or "fans," as Ben & Jerry's terms them). Their evangelists also broadcast their message to new customers far better than any advertising ever could. This strong business position has been made possible via their ethics, values, and activism. At the same time, they aren't hindered by relying on principled sourcing and/or promoting social justice activism. For all these reasons and more, the new philanthrocapitalism model makes quite a lot of sense.

"YOU CAN HAVE BOTH" COMES TO RESTAURANTS

Critics of companies that put their values first point out philanthrocapitalism pioneers exist in niche markets for high-end products. It's true you can survive even in bad weather sans one of Patagonia's nifty fleece jackets. Likewise, your existence is not threatened by a lack of Ben & Jerry's ice cream, although millions of their fans may disagree. But humans require food to exist, and for the busy US family rushing between school, sports, music lessons and a million other activities, that often means relying on fast food. Contrary to what naysayers may say, the principles extolled by the trailblazers we've featured in this chapter also extend to this vertical.

And the industry revolution began with a single book. Journalist Eric Schlosser published *Fast Food Nation* in 2001, forever altering the sector that now prefers the term *quick service* to *fast food*. Not unlike Upton Sinclair's *The Jungle* (1906), which revealed exploitation in the meat industry, Schlosser's book catalogs the risks and dangers of modern fast food. From the abhorrent conditions of slaughterhouses to the unsavory chemicals added to make French fries such delicious guilty pleasures to the industry's insidious practice of advertising to kids, Schlosser lays it all out. He blew the lid off an industry that millions depend on to feed their families, even correctly forecasting problems with food preparation like E. coli outbreaks.

Much like the philanthrocapitalism pioneers who showed the world they could profit while still being ethical, a new wave of fast food entrepreneurs swept in.

Values-driven, they showed it's possible to create healthier foods without exploding costs and lengthy preparation. Consumers also learned they could have fast affordable food and a healthy meal at the same time. As a result, inspired restaurateurs began advertising organic ingredients and grass-fed beef, items we now see daily in ads and signage. In time, the public began to demand more from eateries, no longer convinced they had to trade quality for price or speed.

Although some massive chains that still dominate the fast food economy improved their practices, there were also backslides. You may remember the infamous viral videos of "pink slime" from 2011. (Pink slime, which was sold as ground beef and used by multiple major restaurant chains, is a product of beef trimmings run through a centrifuge, heated, then treated with ammonia. Not the most appetizing food item in the world, especially when the restaurant down the street is advertising gourmet burgers made from grass-fed cows!)

As the fast food industry rehabilitated its approach, it also adopted other practices common to our trailblazers. For example, Shake Shack publishes transparency reports on its website addressing issues such as its animal welfare policy and its commitment to protecting the environment. Similarly, Midwest chain Culver's serves a never-frozen burger free from antibiotics. It also took a page out of The Body Shop's playbook by putting the focus on its suppliers. Since 2013 the company has donated $3.5 million to agricultural education writing on its website, "We're passionate about sharing our appreciation for farmers with guests so they feel connected, investing in agricultural education to ensure the next generation of agricultural leaders is engaged and capable, and supporting climate-smart agricultural efforts that produce nutritious food for a sustainably vibrant food supply."

There can be no doubt the values-driven approach to business is spreading, and we're seeing its aftershocks not only in how companies do business but also in how employees approach their jobs. A recent *Changing Our World* report titled "The Authenticity Opportunity" showed when people believe a company's citizenship claims are authentic the following happens:

- 73% of employees will recommend the company as a good place to work.
- 64% of employees will consider working at the company longer.
- 59% of employees will put in extra effort while working for the company.

WORKERS ARE NOW VALUES-DRIVEN, TOO

Anyone who has worked long enough has seen someone quit in disgust. Not the careful resignation to start a new job, but the dramatic walkout often accompanied by an email manifesto telling the boss off for workplace toxicity. When this happened 20 years ago, it was typically an isolated incident. Nowadays, individual employees benefit from *network* support. Due to social media's rise, an organization's dirty laundry is likely to be aired in a public forum such as Reddit, affecting many others. As a result, it's not uncommon for the crushing weight of peer pressure to exert a force on vast employee populations, especially as millions of strangers converse on Twitter and Facebook.

Anthony Klotz, professor of management at Texas A&M University, coined the term *Great Resignation* to describe the sustained mass quitting of workers in part wrought by the digital hive mind. Others have called it the *Big Quit* or the *Great Reshuffle*, but the idea is the same. Workers are no longer satisfied with trading their values and ethics for a paycheck. Whether it is poor treatment of themselves and coworkers, toxic behavior by managers, or unethical business practices, employees are choosing to leave rather than be employed in a negative situation. And they are getting harder and harder to replace, because they are speaking out on multiple platforms.

Besides the PR nightmare of a Twitter thread detailing nefarious corporate practices, workers can tap into a slew of digital channels to discuss what led them to exit their job. There's LinkedIn, the social network for professionals. There's also Glassdoor, where current and former employees give candid reviews aimed at informing potential hires what they're in for.

Let's extrapolate for a moment. Imagine a prospective employee researching your company before a job interview and reading a message that says, "I quit because the company depends on suppliers in China using forced labor. When I raised the issue to my VP, he told me to 'worry about such things on my own time.'" That's no recipe to attract and retain top talent. It also reveals that more companies are finding prospective employees unwilling to swallow their values in exchange for a compensation package. Crucially, if they don't adjust their style and practices, they'll likely continue to lose their best people to the conscientious company down the street that puts its values first. All these factors contributed to a major shift in corporate America. The writing was on the wall for CEOs for years, but things came to a head in 2019.

CORPORATE AMERICA REDEFINED

The Business Roundtable is a nonprofit lobbyist association bringing together the heads of major companies. In 2019, 181 CEOs from 3M to Walmart united to make a major statement— nothing short of a redefinition of a corporation's stated purpose. But before we explain the shift, let's describe the previous status quo. The legacy purpose of a corporation, one embraced by the Business Roundtable for decades, was to maximize shareholders' return. Actually, this is still the major focus in the minds of many an investor. But America's CEOs have witnessed a cultural shift sparked by innovative companies, adopted by numerous organizations, not to mention its employees, and their customers.

The Business Roundtable addressed the change in a 2019 letter stating that companies should not only serve their shareholders but also other groups such as consumers, workers, suppliers, and the communities in which they operate.

Essentially, it announced a shift toward *stakeholder capitalism*. Stakeholder capitalism is a management theory taking into consideration not only the best interests of a company overall or its shareholders but also the many groups and individuals a company works with. Included in this constituency are employees and suppliers, but it can also extend to the environment and other areas traditionally considered special interests. What's more, stakeholder capitalism addresses morals, values, and missions beyond profit and shareholder return. (If this sounds familiar, that's because stakeholder capitalism has been practiced by companies such as Patagonia, Ben & Jerry's, and The Body Shop for decades.)

The Business Roundtable describes the change in these terms:

> America's economic model, which is based on freedom, liberty, and other enduring principles of our democracy, has raised standards of living for generations, while promoting competition, consumer choice and innovation. America's businesses have been a critical engine to its success.
>
> Yet we know that many Americans are struggling. Too often hard work is not rewarded, and not enough is being done for workers to adjust to the rapid pace of change in the economy. If companies fail to recognize that the success of our system is dependent on inclusive long-term growth, many will raise legitimate questions about the role of large employers in our society.

The organization also detailed those stakeholders corporations must serve, notably listing shareholders *last*. Their list includes these actions:

- Delivering value to our customers

- Investing in our employees

- Dealing fairly and ethically with our suppliers

- Supporting the communities in which we work

- Generating long-term value for shareholders

The fact that 181 CEOs from the largest US companies could unite and agree to this list demonstrates just how far we've come from traditional definitions of corporate responsibility based on profit and loss. Still, this newfound dedication to values would introduce a variety of ethical problems in the coming years. For example, can a company profess its virtue and ethical treatment of employees when its electronic products are made in sweatshops?

That's a tough question, one that's beyond our book's purview. Still, the good news for companies seeking to do better is that new organizational breeds are popping up to help companies give back better. One such group is the 1% Pledge, encouraging members to return 1% of their time, equity, profit, or product to charitable causes. This global movement has signed up more than 10,000 members in 100 countries, generating more than $500 million in philanthropy. Not bad!

WHAT THIS MEANS FOR NONPROFITS

Corporate America's latest edicts indicate it isn't enough to just make billions in profits. Businesses must commit to improving outcomes for *all* stakeholders, whether that's creating better workplaces for employees, establishing fairer deals with suppliers, or promising not to harm the environment. As some of the original trailblazers demonstrated, these laudable efforts can lead to, yes, *higher revenues* but also better relationships with staff and other stakeholders, as well as deep loyalty from consumers who resonate with a brand (that Radical Connection we've been mentioning).

This all sounds great, but there's one problem—the unintended consequences of this new corporate attitude on nonprofits. Think back to the story of Jamal and his Tesla at the beginning of this chapter. In years past, Jamal gave money to organizations such as the Sierra Club and Greenpeace because he cared deeply about the environment. Now, he gets the same positive feelings by buying a Tesla. On a smaller scale, a consumer may pursue altruistic actions by purchasing a pair of TOMS shoes, knowing that a third of the profits will go to community efforts, driving sustainable change.

This begs a difficult question: Is buying products and services from companies with a positive mission the new charity? Most likely—unless nonprofits learn from corporations. Fast. Without such intervention, in the coming years we'll likely see more people, especially younger individuals, checking off the proverbial "giving box" by making purchases from companies with clear missions and strong values emphasizing shared causes.

Accordingly, the conventional thinking of such consumers will dictate that if they have "mindfully" invested their money in companies and products that are ethically produced and contribute to a greater mission, further action is not necessary. Like Jamal, these consumers will think to themselves that they have purchased food grown by local farmers, wear clothing ethically sourced, and drive a car that doesn't contribute to air pollution. They'll ask, "What more can I do?"

The losers in this logic, of course, are the many nonprofits relying on charitable gifts to complete their vital work. We do not deny the importance of more companies adopting stakeholder capitalism. We consider it a benefit for the world if more businesses become mission-centric, wishing to do good. However, there is a clear danger that this emerging model will decrease traditional notions of generosity. Even worse, it reduces the engagement the public has toward nonprofits—a concept we will soon cover as Radical Connection—critical to continuing a tradition of generosity well into the future.

Left unchecked, corporate societal efforts could unintendedly exacerbate the Generosity Crisis just as severely as the external and internal factors listed in the previous chapter. This could create other unintended negative consequences, such as allowing corporations to set the agendas for the entire country, lessening the impact of nonprofits in their communities and harming our world. On a related note, consumers may vote with their dollars by funding companies with missions they support but will otherwise have little say in that mission. In practice, Musk will decide when SpaceX rockets fly to Mars, with or without the input of those who buy his cars. Just this one example shows us how we will soon be even more subject to the whims of the business strategists if nonprofits are weakened by corporations' ability to not just sell a product but also tap into your personal values.

WHY THE CORPORATIONS TOOK ACTION

A wide variety of surveys and polls show Americans are a generous people, an unchanging characteristic of our culture for years. But savvy corporations also recognized they could scratch the generosity itch in many consumers with an ethically made Patagonia sweater or an exhaust-free Tesla car. In a similar fashion of doing good, younger generations now seek new ways to improve the world. Fortunately, a vast menu of generosity options has exploded in the 21st century. Because of this, many people feel like they are giving back in new ways that aren't being counted yet in the same way.

This new reality cannot help but promote some uneasy soul searching.

No matter their age, many people may be prone to ask, "It feels good to do good, but *am I really doing good?*" Ultimately, the hard work of corporations has paid off. Many consumers now see themselves as virtuous and as effective at improving the world as the many nonprofits in their community. But the corporations' move wasn't just due to shifting consumer sentiment; their timing was based on a far more negative trend. Our collective trust in each other and our institutions has plummeted, and companies are swooping in to fill that void, too. This is the subject of Chapter 4.

CHAPTER **4**

The Trust Breakdown

What would you do with a million dollars? Anyone who has ever bought a lotto ticket has a plan for that first million. It usually involves paying off debts, buying new vehicles, and/or taking a long vacation somewhere nice—maybe somewhere exotic. Likewise, many Americans have an even more expansive fantasy of what they'd do if they came into $10 million or even $100 million. This varies from person to person but might involve early retirement or buying a business that could evolve into a winning family legacy. Philanthropy is not top of mind for most people; in fact, statistics from GoBankingRates confirm "that only 7% of respondents said the first thing they would do if they won the lottery is donate their winnings to charity."

Now once you get into what you do with *billions*, the answers from most non-billionaires become hazy. It's difficult to conceive of $20 billion, let alone imagine what you might do with such an incredible sum.

A Tale of Two Moguls

Of course, some billionaires buy toys, just like everyday individuals who make their first million. One famous example is the recent boat purchase of Amazon founder Jeff Bezos. As of this writing, Bezos is the world's second richest person. What do you do when your personal wealth exceeds the GDP of more than 50 countries? You acquire the world's largest yacht, naturally, and let no obstacle stand in your way—including historic bridges.

Bezos's new superyacht is an incredible vessel, at 417 feet long, and Bloomberg estimates it costs more than $500 million. To put the size of this seacraft in perspective, it comes with its own *companion yacht* for getting around easier. The super yacht is under construction in the Dutch city of Rotterdam, but yacht builder Oceanco realized not long ago that they had hit a snag. Bezos's new flagship was too big to sail out to the ocean. The historic Koningshaven Bridge, a Rotterdam landmark, blocked it.

The bridge, commonly referred to by locals as De Hef, was built in 1927 and repaired after it was damaged in World War II. To appease Bezos, the bridge was to be dismantled to allow the mighty superyacht to sail through on its maiden journey. Now, as you can imagine, many locals were outraged by this plan, including more than 4,000 according to NPR Dutch citizens who expressed interest in a Facebook event organizing people to pelt the superyacht with rotten eggs as it passed the bridge. The point of this story isn't to comment on Bezos's choice in nautical travel. Rather, it's to illustrate that when a person reaches this unimaginable wealth level, the world's largest yacht doesn't put a strain on their finances. Likewise, the prospect of dismantling a historic bridge is reduced to a small inconvenience.

But not every billionaire is notable for their travel habits. Some prefer real estate. One such real estate mogul is Meta's (aka Facebook) founder Mark Zuckerberg, with an estimated fortune of $68.6 billion, according to *Forbes* as of May 2022. Zuckerberg is the youngest person in the top 20 billionaires list and the only one under 40. His real estate interests are centered on a veritable paradise. Recently, he purchased about 1,300 acres on the Hawaiian island of Kauai. (Fans of *Jurassic Park* would be interested to know most of the original film was shot here, specifically because of its pristine beaches and unspoiled forests.)

As it so happens, Zuckerberg makes Hawaii his primary home. And similar to Bezos, he has faced criticism over his practices on the island. In 2017 Zuckerberg filed multiple lawsuits against native Hawaiians, trying to force them to sell their land parcels to "enhance" his estate's privacy. Even after dropping the controversial lawsuits, the *New York Post* reports Zuckerberg kept up his acquisition campaign, this time by using a third-party buyer to pressure the landholders. Also, similar to Bezos and his leviathan yacht, even Zuckerberg's massive Hawaii land grab fails to make a dent in his outsized fortune. Possessing the means, he made the decision, as many billionaires have before him, to steer his wealth toward philanthropic causes.

Yet *how* he's done so tells us much about the future of giving in America.

PHILANTHROPY REIMAGINED

Mark Zuckerberg and his wife, Priscilla Chan, have pledged to donate 99% of their lifetime worth, but they didn't follow traditional avenues to do so. For instance, they didn't partner with charitable organizations. Nor did they form a trust or even a private foundation to go about their philanthropy. Instead, Zuckerberg formed the Chan Zuckerberg Initiative (CZI) as an LLC.

This decision left many onlookers with the same question: why an LLC?

As it turns out, the CZI was funded with an estimated $45 billion, mostly in the form of Facebook shares. As *Forbes* explains, by choosing to exist as a limited liability company instead of private foundation or charitable trust, the CZI can do things nonprofits can't, such as invest in for-profits, make political donations, and avoid the transparency rules of various forms of nonprofits. (Also, Zuckerberg remains in control of the Facebook shares held by the CZI, maintaining tight reins over the company he founded and still leads today.)

Now let's consider the CZI's mission. Focused on improving education, it prioritizes housing and economic opportunities, as well as promotes scientific research. Politics was also a major focus area until 2020, when CZI announced it would no longer fund campaigns directly.

THE PUBLIC RESPONDS

Since its inception, the CZI organization has enjoyed widespread praise. Daniel Lurie, founder of the poverty-fighting charity Tipping Point, once said, "Seeing Mark Zuckerberg and Priscilla Chan commit such a large percentage of their wealth at such a young age promotes the urgency of the issues of poverty we see all around us. These problems are simply too big to wait."

Despite such acclaim, the CZI is not immune to criticism. *ProPublica* reporter Jesse Eisinger was quick to point out untoward benefits of the CZI's design in a social media post: "And because Zuckerberg's thing is an LLC, he can give to political organizations, SuperPACs, all that stuff, w/ money that was never taxed." Eisinger then expanded on his thinking in an article published by *The New York Times*, writing, "A charitable foundation is subject to rules and oversight. It has to allocate a certain percentage of its assets every year. The new Zuckerberg LLC won't be subject to those rules and won't have any transparency requirements."

Corporate tax expert Robert Willens also perceived problems with the LLC. He told *CBS News* that "the donation has been characterized a little too simplistically as an outright charitable donation of 99 percent of his wealth. Certainly, it could wind up being that if he directed all of the LLC's funds to charity, but the jury is still out regarding what percentage of his wealth will be directed to charity."

This case is yet another example of how traditional philanthropy (our Generosity Crisis) differs from the ability and options people seeking societal impact possess today. Certainly, Mark Zuckerberg has proven to be a business visionary. There is little doubt he will be emulated by others copying his model of setting up an LLC for philanthropic ventures. The risk is that if *other* billionaires, especially from the tech sector, follow this lead, they, too, may be less inclined to participate in traditional philanthropy. In fact, we're likely to see CZI copycats spring up, even if they aren't of the same size or sophistication.

WHY THIS MATTERS

Trust is the currency of nonprofit organizations. The rationale precipitating Zuckerberg's iconoclastic move and that of so many inevitable copycats to come boils down to one thing: trust. Trust, once so fundamental to nonprofits, has collapsed in recent years. At the same time, corporations have swooped in to fill the gap. Plenty of experts in the nonprofit economy acknowledge the trust gap's existence, yet few understand the problem's true extent. It's a five-alarm fire. People just know don't it yet. How bad have things gotten? A 2022 bombshell from PR powerhouse firm Edelman offers a stark revelation or just reveals: "Trust in governments and media has been steadily declining for over a decade, with *businesses* now the most trusted source of information" (emphasis ours).

The shocker came from the 2022 Edelman Trust Barometer, the annual trust and credibility survey administered by the public relations firm. The data underlying it arises from a robust set of interviews; 36,000 respondents from 28 countries measured trust among various domains—corporate, nonprofit, government, and media—by examining many factors, including ethics and competency. The report's only bright spot? Nonprofits are *still* perceived to be more ethical than their for-profit counterparts. The rest bodes quite negatively for the future of nonprofits.

SEA CHANGE

The Edelman Barometer shows us an inescapable—and unprecedented—truth: for-profit organizations have boosted their perceived competency to the level they are now viewed as more trustworthy than nonprofits. The implications of this cannot be overstated. This is the first time in the survey's 22-year history that corporations achieved such a pronounced victory over their nonprofit counterparts. Of course, this is in part due to corporations' ability to execute highly prescriptive and sustained marketing strategies and the positive cultural shift associated with these companies. (This is the subject of our previous chapter.) Who can blame someone for thinking that buying a Tesla is a better way to save the environment than donating to charities?

Yet from another perspective, there are many inefficient nonprofits that have unfortunately damaged the reputation of this economy.

WHAT DISTRUST IN NONPROFITS LOOKS AND FEELS LIKE

There is a tendency in any industry for the worst bad actors to spoil things for everyone. This is true in medicine. For years, quacks and charlatans peddled their version of snake oil or engaged in serial malpractice. Such chicanery set back the medical industry, provoking distrust. Here's a recent example of poor public perception affecting a medical company. Before 1982, Tylenol enjoyed the distinction of being the industry leader in pain relief with its parent company Johnson & Johnson (J&J) enjoying nearly 40% market share.

Then in fall 1982 someone replaced Tylenol extra-strength capsules with cyanide, a lethal poison, on the shelves of several pharmacies and stores. This malicious act led to the death of seven unsuspecting individuals. Immediately, J&J flew into action. After alerting the public to the health crisis, they told consumers not to buy any more of their products until it could determine other bottles of the medicine had not been tampered with. J&J also ceased production and advertising, ordering a national recall.

The seriousness with which the company took the crisis and its willingness to protect consumers from future dangers more than restored public confidence in the brand. It went from losing major trust to regaining major trust, due to its transparent and persistent efforts to fix the problem, even if that meant suffering significant financial losses. According to https://www.ou.edu/deptcomm, "The Tylenol crisis is without a doubt the most exemplary case ever known in the history of crisis communications. Any business executive, who has ever stumbled into a public relations ambush, ought to appreciate the way Johnson & Johnson responded to the Tylenol poisonings. They have effectively demonstrated how major business has to handle a disaster."

Of course, the nonprofit sector is also susceptible to the same slings and arrows. Regular warnings about charity scams and wasteful nonprofits bombard the public. The ensuing negative outcome is due in part to modern tech. Sites such as GoFundMe have (often unwittingly) made scams easier than ever to pull off. Yet even when the maligned subjects of these articles are in fact bad actors—and not the group itself—the damage is done. Their poor example casts widespread dispersion on their organization, not to mention the industry in general, enabling a drumbeat of distrust. This invokes suspicion toward nonprofits writ large, even in the hearts of the most giving Americans.

GOING TO THE DARK SIDE

Let's examine the tone of one revealing article on this subject to understand just how trust in nonprofits has collapsed in recent years. Consumer finance reporter Allen Lee published a piece on the website Money Inc in 2019 titled "The 20 Worst Charities You Shouldn't Be Donating To."

Lee broke down many notorious nonprofits' practices, stating in his introduction that "most philanthropic foundations do exactly what they advertise on the tin." The first example on Lee's list is the Cancer Fund of America. We are including his description of the organization in full because it is instructive as to how distrust of one group can inflict harm on others.

Cancer Fund of America is just one of many philan-thropic centers run by James T. Reynolds and his some-what crooked family. That the no-shame Reynolds takes home an annual salary of around $230,000 is bad enough (and properly tells you all you need to know about where your donations are going). That the char-ity (and we mean "charity" in the loosest possible sense) only manages to find it in its heart to give 2.5% of its donations to support the families of cancer victims and fund cancer research (its supposed raison d'etre) is even worse. If you want to subsidize the flash lifestyle of

Reynolds, then go right ahead and donate. If you'd rather your money found its way into the pockets of who it should, then maybe find yourself a better cause.

What's immediately evident from this passage is its vitriolic tone. It drips with disdain. This is a by-product of clickbait online journalism where articles feature dramatic language to keep readers engaged. Still, it conveys growing and palpable distrust for nonprofits all the same. There was a time when nonprofits held the proverbial "moral high ground." These days, charities and philanthropic organizations are subject to the skepticism, suspicion, and scrutiny for-profit corporations have long faced, if not more, as corporations have become ever more trusted in recent years. Next, Lee's criticism isn't just a judgment of the organization's style or (in)ability to achieve its mission. It's also an examination of its financial metrics, such as the percentage of donations that reach their intended target. Whatever we think about Lee's toxic prose, he knows his audience. He's aware consumers are becoming ever savvier concerning financial details. They no longer blindly trust nonprofits to do the right thing. "Trust but verify" might be a charitable way to put such mentality. (No pun intended.) In essence, they want to see the books.

It Gets Worse

Lee goes on to indict other charities engendering distrust. He highlights a nonprofit named the Children's Wish Foundation, claiming it may have been founded to purposefully cause confusion with the Make-A-Wish Foundation. To this point, *Consumer Reports* quotes Bennett Weiner of the BBB Wise Giving Alliance, who explains, "In some cases, soundalike charities are there with the intent to deceive donors into thinking they are donating to somebody else."

Now, what could possibly cause more distrust and confusion among well-meaning donors than a slew of similarly named charities? After all, a donor wants to feel they are doing the right thing and moving a mission they care passionately about forward. They have no interest in contributing to some knockoff organization purposely bent on obfuscating its name for dollars.

Other dangers surround names, producing more distrust, for instance, when the names are essentially identical. Lee takes aim at Project Cure (Florida), which he claims does little to advance its goal of public knowledge and awareness on serious topical illnesses. When Lee suggests donating to other charities in its place, he writes, "The Project Cures in Ohio and Colorado (neither of which are associated with their Florida namesake) represent two such possibilities." Who knew that along with Charity Navigator, a donor had to keep Google Maps open at the same time?

Exploiting Desperate Times Doesn't Make Things Any Better

Unfortunately, growing distrust is even more extreme during periods of duress, such as the 2022 Russian invasion of Ukraine. The war raging as we write this book has left many Ukrainians in need of immediate aid, and generous Americans have rallied to their cause.

There's just one problem.

Most have no clue whom they can trust. NPR reports Americans and Europeans have been inundated with crowdfunding campaigns, appeals, and charity drives to support Ukrainian refugees, with little ability to discern legitimate organizations from scams. Bennett Weiner explains: "When people try and take advantage of generous donors, they're going to do so when the emotion runs high and the heat of the moment. And that's mainly after disasters and tragedies—things of that nature when people are motivated to give." Weiner then shares his advice on making (helpful) donations to Ukraine: "Established relief organizations are your best bet. Many of them already have presences in the area, and they know the type of assistance they need to provide."

Let's talk about how to get this right. *The Washington Post* reported back in March 2022 how the corporation Airbnb helped the war efforts in an ingenious way, by booking rooms on Airbnb with proceeds aiding Ukrainians:

> Mak [a paying guest] is among thousands of people using Airbnb as an immediate and intimate way to help those living through war in Ukraine. On Wednesday and Thursday, more than 61,000 nights were booked in Ukraine from people around the world, according to an Airbnb spokesman, who added that the total booking value was nearly $2 million.
>
> The company late last week waived all guest and host fees on bookings in Ukraine and said that operations in Russia and Belarus were suspended. Last Monday, Airbnb announced it was offering "free, short-term housing to up to 100,000 refugees fleeing Ukraine," according to a news release.

Clearly, positive outreach efforts such as this contribute to widespread feelings of trust corporations already enjoy. Now, let's return to some of the less-than-ethical nonprofits sullying the reputation of the industry. How can a donor ever be sure they are giving to an established organization when a scam startup may have a similar moniker, and the solicitor is an

experienced operator used to convincing targets of a false connection with an established nonprofit? During an international
crisis such as the war in Ukraine, it's like shooting fish in a barrel
for the bad guys.

This isn't only happening in the US either; it is also a major
problem in the United Kingdom. An article titled "Deplorable
scam emails fake fundraising for Ukraine" published by the BBC
on March 23, 2022, describes a situation as confusing and filled
with fraud as the one playing out in the states.

"The UK's national fraud reporting centre is warning about
fake emails pretending to raise money for victims of the war in
Ukraine. Action Fraud has received 196 reports of bogus requests
to fundraise for victims of the crisis." As it turns out, scammers
are using tricks such as selling T-shirts and even stealing the
names and likenesses of prominent Ukrainians to trick the trust-
ing public into handing over their money. They are making a
quick buck at the expense of US and English donors (not to mention Ukrainians in desperate need of aid!) while also causing lasting damage to the future ability of nonprofits to raise precious
funds, no matter their efficiency and/or effectiveness.

Just consider the measures donors are expected to take to
avoid fraud in this uncertain environment. In a November 2019
Consumer Reports article on gifting to nonprofits, author Penelope
Wang lays out safeguards that donors should take before signing
a check or swiping their credit card. Some tips include verifying
a group's IRS tax-exempt status, giving directly instead of to a
fundraiser, double-checking for credit card fees, and requesting
privacy from future solicitations.

In the past, all this work might have been associated with
buying a used car from a sleazy dealer, not donating to a cause

someone feels passionately about. More important, these devel-
opments portend clear storm clouds on the horizon for every
nonprofit in America. *The Chronicle of Philanthropy* reported on
other potential troubles that nonprofits will soon need to shoulder based on rising distrust levels in a January 2020 article by
Ben Gose titled "The Trust Crisis." Gose writes, "As trust in
nonprofits sinks to new lows, charitable organizations could face
many threats to their ability to carry out their missions, including trouble raising cash, attracting top talent, and persuading
Americans to take action on social, environmental, and other
key issues."

Of course, all of these are significant challenges, but diffi-
culty raising cash is of particular importance considering our
larger Generosity Crisis. Think about a charity-minded person
who wants to help but has also taken *Consumer Reports*' advice to
heart. They would love to donate, but between two children with
sports practices and a high-pressure job, who has time to search
the IRS website for an organization's present tax status or efficiency rating? Inevitably, when distrust waxes, donations wane.

THE CORPORATE GAME PLAN: BE MISSION-DRIVEN AND COLLECT BIG DATA

It may seem incomprehensible that for-profit companies are now
more trusted than governments and even nonprofits. Even if we
don't want to admit it, it is the truth. And we documented the
reasons why in the previous chapter. Put simply, corporations
have taken a page out of nonprofits' playbook to understand the
value of connection by becoming more mission-driven. (In many
cases, it would be more accurate to say they *took the entire book*—
then added deep consumer insights powered by big data and artificial intelligence to it as an appendix.)

To return to one of the corporate trailblazers detailed in Chapter 3, Ben & Jerry's serves as an excellent example of how trust has flip-flopped between corporations and nonprofits. In fact, many Americans mistakenly believe the Vermont-based ice cream manufacturer is *itself a nonprofit* with a commercial ice cream business attached. (This is much like how the Girl Scouts of America aren't a cookie company, but a nonprofit fueling its mission via sales of Thin Mints and Tagalongs.)

Nevertheless, this erroneous belief stems from the company's social activism and public stance on current events and issues such as prison reform, social justice, and the Israeli-Palestinian conflict. The Vermont-based outfit also moves quickly on social issues. It frequently comes out with an ice cream flavor tied to a particular cause, pledging a portion of proceeds to it, such as the Black Lives Matter movement, while the cause is still in the headlines. Some Ben & Jerry's fans might be even more confused to learn their favorite activist company is actually owned by global megacorporation Unilever.

Now, if consumers supporting Ben & Jerry's and similar companies are struggling to distinguish them from nonprofits due to their mission-driven approach to capitalism, the opposite is true about the corporations themselves. They have gained a precise understanding of their customers—thanks to the power of big data. Twenty years ago, Ben & Jerry's might have possessed the same level of knowledge about a particular person as a non-profit. (Actually less, because the typical Ben & Jerry's fan likely purchased ice cream from different shops and only kept in touch by signing up for the company's mailing list.) Yet as big data became the world's most valuable commodity, these companies gained a vast understanding of its customers far outstripping what most nonprofits currently know about its donors and/or prospects.

These days, big data, as harnessed by corporations through highly personalized algorithms, helps them gain specific insights into not only general consumer behavior but also us as *individuals*. This goes way beyond scanning a loyalty card at the grocery store or using an app to get restaurant reward points. This is about tech companies gobbling up intel about everything you see, say, type, or search, then turning it into content sold to advertisers and brands. Basically, if you use a digital platform or an app and aren't paying for it directly, there's a strong chance you're paying for it another way—with personal details from your life.

Security.org details this immense data collection in an article titled "The Data Big Tech Companies Have on You." Notably, the article gives Google, the largest internet company on earth, a dismal grade of F for the sheer volume it collects of its users. Google knows who you are, where you are, what you like to look at, what you enjoy eating for dinner on Tuesdays, even who you think is cute in the office. Worse yet, the data is all up for sale, as documented in a recent report by the Irish Council for Civil Liberties, documenting how Google auctions data on its users to corporations around the world.

According to the report:

The data can go to dozens or even hundreds of companies for each auction. Google says it transmits the data of American users to about 4,700 companies in total across the world. Each "broadcast"—as they are called in the industry—typically shares data about a person's location—including "hyperlocal" targeting, according to Google('s) own pitch to advertisers—personal characteristics and browsing habits to help ad firms build user profiles. The ad industry also has a lengthy taxonomy that the networks use to categorize people, including sensitive labels like "anxiety disorders" and "legal issues," or even "incest" and "abuse support," according to a public document published by the ad network consortium that sets standards for the industry.

Based on this information, it makes sense that consumers would find themselves in a closer relationship with for-profit companies when the latter can categorize them as abuse survivors (for advertising purposes) thanks to Google. The result of this emerging paradigm? Due to mission-driven capitalism and big data, nonprofits are being squeezed out even more, which results in less mind share, emotional share, and wallet share. As if this wasn't a big enough issue, it's led to a secondary problem, something we broached in Chapter 2. Corporations suddenly possess massive power to drive agendas. A generation ago it was well-placed individuals leading the philanthropic crusade. Not so much anymore.

The math says it all. Take the massive resources at a corporation's disposal and add in growing public distrust. The result? An overshadowing of small and medium-sized nonprofits and their honorable work to improve our world. So, what happens when the richest, most powerful companies influence philanthropy without partnership? Well, we've already seen one such sample and it didn't work out well for anyone—especially math students. We're referring to corporate mogul Bill Gates and his championing of Common Core in education.

WHAT COMMON CORE CAN TEACH US (EVEN IF IT DIDN'T TEACH THE KIDS)

Bill Gates is widely known as the founder of Microsoft, but he has a variety of other interesting titles to his name. For one, he's now the largest owner of farmland in the country. Along with his many investments, Gates became active in philanthropy long before next-gen Silicon Valley tycoons such as Mark Zuckerberg. The Bill & Melinda Gates Foundation has varied missions, including improving medical care and nutrition in developing countries and education here at home. Possessing an endowment valued at more than $50 billion, the Bill & Melinda Gates Foundation enjoys more assets than any other US institution. Since its inception, it's also distributed more than $60 billion to causes tied to eradicating diseases and reducing global poverty.

Well intentioned, Gates's involvement in the Common Core boondoggle is nonetheless an apt illustration of what can go wrong when corporations or their leaders are driving social agendas on their own. Common Core was developed as a plan to standardize goals in US public school classrooms. It meant to end massive variations in standards between states so a high school diploma from one state could safely be expected to mean the same thing as one from another.

This is how the initiative's own website describes it:

> The Common Core State Standards Initiative is a state-led effort coordinated by the National Governors Association Center for Best Practices (NGA Center) and the Council of Chief State School Officers (CCSSO). The standards were developed in collaboration with teachers, school administrators, and experts to provide a clear and consistent framework to prepare our children for college and the workforce.

The education advocates behind Common Core thought they had the right plan to get the US on track, but they needed someone with national prominence and a seemingly bottomless checkbook to overcome traditional politics between states. Okay, let's be honest, it's almost impossible to get all 50 states and the District of Columbia to agree on *anything*, let alone a touchy subject such as educational standards. To achieve this goal, the architects of Common Core turned to Bill and Melinda Gates in a 2008 Seattle meeting. To say they joined the cause with gusto would be the understatement of the year—and where Bill Gates's passion goes, his money follows.

Gates, the richest man in the world at the time, was an immediate convert to the cause. What's more, he had the financial muscle to move mountains, or in this case, get states to work together harmoniously. Gates poured hundreds of millions of dollars, with most estimates ranging between $200 and $400 million, into pushing the Common Core mission. In the same way Jeff Bezos tried to have a historic bridge dismantled because it was in the way of his new yacht, Gates paid to overcome challenges to Common Core.

Gates critic and public school teacher Mercedes Schneider, writing for *HuffPost*, quipped, "[Common Core] is not 'state led.' It is 'Gates led.' How foolish it is to believe that the man with the checkbook is not calling the CCSS shots." Further criticizing Gates, Schneider characterized him as "one man, lots of money, nationally shaping a profession to which he has never belonged."

And nationally shape the profession of education is what Gates did. As *The Washington Post* reported in a June 7, 2014, article on Gates and Common Core, "The result was astounding: Within just two years of the 2008 Seattle meeting, 45 states and the District of Columbia had fully adopted the Common Core State Standards." In the era before corporations and tech billionaires directed philanthropy from on high, nonprofits would fill education gaps by providing expertise in areas such as math, literacy, and other fields in which public schools were failing our children, especially underprivileged kids. Instead, Gates led and funded a rush into Common Core, which has been conclusively proven to be a tragic failure based on six years of data.

Common Core's flop is indisputable when the evidence is reviewed, as it was by influential educator Theodor Rebarber in a white paper called "The Common Core Debacle" published by the Pioneer Institute in 2020. Rebarber's analysis showed the average annual gain in math scores for both fourth and eighth graders dropped in the Common Core era after several years of trending upward. Ironically, Common Core was most damaging to the lowest-achieving students it was supposed to lift up. Pupils at the 25th and 10th percentiles lagged further behind than ever. Rebarber described this disappointment, saying, "The sustained decline we're now seeing, especially among our most vulnerable students, simply cannot be allowed to continue."

Although Common Core is a national program, the real tragedy of its failure is most visible at the state level. As *National Review* explains in an article concerning Rebarber's white paper, pre–Common Core Massachusetts had a sterling record of K–12 education performance. For years, the state's schools finished first in every category on The Nation's Report Card, the National Assessment of Educational Progress (NAEP). Following Common Core implementation, the state now shows the steepest decline rate in multiple subjects. Despite good intentions, Massachusetts swapped the best-performing schools in the nation for fastest-declining schools, fueled by Gates's money.

Gates himself has acknowledged the fiasco. In a 2017 speech, he said, "If there is one thing I have learned, it is that no matter how enthusiastic we might be about one approach or another, the decision to go from pilot to wide-scale usage is ultimately and always something that has to be decided by you and others the field." That might be what Gates learned, but what we can learn is corporations applying their resources to social problems will not necessarily result in better results than when nonprofits do it—*but the public trusts them to.*

As discussed, Musk and the new class of socially conscious corporate leaders have no qualms associating their business with philanthropy. Musk explicitly ties Tesla with the goal of saving the environment. Because people trust these corporations, it leads them to believe the way to give back to society is by also fulfilling their own desires for a new car (or ice cream, or whatever else they desire). Whether it's Gates, Musk, or Ben & Jerry's, the case for Radical Connection—when people with financial means work in close partnership with key programs and services being delivered—offers the chance for strong partnerships between corporations and nonprofits. We will see this in action in Chapter 10 via our interview with John Damonti, president of Bristol Myers Squibb Foundation.

For now, the ability of companies to win public trust and agenda set speaks directly to the Generosity Crisis we face. Already, the average American wrestles with how to spend their discretionary income in an over-commercialized society. Providing them yet another way to spend money on themselves—and feel good about it—is absolutely a winning business model for corporations, and a losing one for traditional philanthropy.

This may all sound a bit grim. And we haven't yet tackled the biggest problem of all, the troubling development most responsible for the crisis: the breakdown of human connections. Vital to the successful missions of nonprofits, rekindling these connections is the major focus of the second half of this book. But don't fret! It's always darkest before dawn. After one more chapter on the pressing challenges nonprofits face, we will turn to solutions.

CHAPTER 5

The Continental Connection Drift

Filmmakers Jamin and Kiowa Winans and Robert Muratore released the eye-opening documentary *Childhood 2.0* in 2020. The film, which should be required viewing for every parent, dives into the dangers of our cultural obsession with social media and a perpetually online culture. From the dangers of ubiquitous pornography and online predators to suicidal ideation among teens (and even younger) the film documents a disturbing breakdown in human connection. Through interviews with parents and children we get a firsthand view of how living online has changed childhood forever.

Surprisingly for a movie that focuses on cutting-edge tech and social media, the film also reveals the atomization of US culture by capturing the story of a woman now in her 80s. As a retired special education teacher and grandmother, Doris Gosnell explains in *Childhood 2.0*, being born in the height of the Great Depression meant everyone had to contribute and coexist for the family to survive. The bonds of connection were existentially vital.

Let's consider how her experience parallels—and diverges—from that of kids today.

A Tale of Two Childhoods

Unlike many modern US kids, Doris grew up fast. Much was expected from her. She had significant roles and responsibilities. From a young age, she contributed to the chores of farm life. She also kept herself busy so as not to burden her anxious parents with her care. She accomplished this by playing outside with a group composed of siblings and neighbor children who would often stay out from sunrise to sundown.

These little boys and girls went through good times and bad times. *Together.* When there wasn't quite enough food to eat, they shared their meager lunches, pretending it was a great feast. They spoke to each other often and always face-to-face, describing their fears but also their hopes and dreams, paying rapt attention to the way their words and actions affected the other. Tellingly, celebrating birthdays and holidays with her friends in this deep fashion created more vivid memories than any lavish celebration Doris would enjoy later in life as the Depression ended and US fortunes lifted.

What Doris was doing in her childhood was creating indelible bonds. Deep connections between others give life meaning. They can also generate memories that are as vivid at age 85 as they were at 10. More than anything, these relationships were Doris's prized possessions. As such, she and her friends cultivated and maintained them all the rest all their days. Certainly, Doris lived in a bygone era, a time vastly different from our own. Yet the rich lives of Doris and her friends are not isolated outliers. The social cohesion their generation enjoyed was once near universal, the typical experience most everyone enjoyed as their human birthright.

In fact, once upon a time, US culture was based on creating precisely these types of vibrant and lasting connections within communities. Decades before social media, remote instruction, and Zoom conferencing, Doris and her friends enjoyed their own primitive version of a "flash mob." It resulted in Doris's marriage. As she explains, 4-H was a big part of her teen years. The youth development organization once occupied an outsized role in young people's social lives. Commonly associated with rural America, it held regular activities to bring teens together to meet each other, socialize, and learn life skills.

Based on her happy experiences in it, Doris also joined Rural Youth, an extension for college-aged young adults. The group brought young people together for dances, hayrides, and other social activities. As Doris explains in *Childhood 2.0*, "There were a lot of marriages, my friend Mary Lou and I both met our husbands through Rural Youth. . . . It's how I met my Mr. Right." Clearly, the deep human connections fostered by organizations like 4-H and Rural Youth played a big role in Doris's upbringing. Without them she would have surely succumbed to despair, isolated and poor as she was, suffering through one of the hardest moments in history.

Now, consider another interview in *Childhood 2.0*, where modern teen girls describe how dating works today. One is asked how she knows "dating" has begun. Her answer: "The guy says you're hot, pretty much." She adds, "The guy will add you on Snapchat, and you might say you like each other, but of course it's over texts, it's not face-to-face." A comparison between vapid pickup lines exchanged from screen to screen via Snapchat to Doris's tale of in-person square dancing (where she met and fell in love with "Mr. Right") is astonishing. The former couldn't be further from Doris's experience. Instead, it typifies a cynical hookup culture where discombobulated avatars interact from screen to screen on the shallowest of terms: "You're hot. I like you." (It's hard to imagine this fleeting connection—if we can even call it that—will induce *any* kind of indelible memory—much less a precious one sustaining itself throughout a lifetime.)

What becomes clear is this insight: Despite the fact Doris and her family lived through the Great Depression, one of the most harrowing periods in US modern history, she and her peers suffered much less actual depression than today's youth—individuals who grew up in a period of extreme material abundance—especially by Doris's standards. Case in point: in the documentary, we learn of a modern young man who took his own life after succumbing to his own despair. (One of many such tragic cases that are on the upswing, unfortunately.)

The interviewer then poses this question to Doris: "Do you remember there being suicides or anything like that [in your day]?"

Without hesitation she shakes her head. "Never. I never have heard that. We were worried, we were more worried about physical illnesses. But I don't remember there being a problem with suicide." (Recall, this is someone who experienced tremendous loss, including the death of beloved siblings at a young age.)

Conversely, America's modern young people needn't worry as much about physical illnesses, at least not the types that ravaged families in the 1920s when the childhood mortality rate (185 out of 1,000 children did not live past 5 years of age) was much higher than it is today (5.4 out of 1,000). In America, today's youth aren't in danger of contracting polio or perishing from starvation (most at least), but they're also not living lives filled with deep personal connection. Instead, as *Childhood 2.0* depicts, they are staying indoors, playing video games, and obsessing over the number of "likes" on their social media profile instead of creating the rich human bonds so emblematic of Doris's generation.

AND THEN COVID MADE THINGS WORSE

Social media and online gaming didn't emerge at the same time as the coronavirus pandemic. Nor did even teleconferencing for work, education, or personal communication. Instead, we were well down the path of isolating young people and separating them from meaningful human connections long before shelter-in-place orders became a common part of the English language.

Another term for such isolation is *atomization*. Columnist Willow Liana wrote a compelling article in March 2020 for the online publication Erraticus.co, titled "All the Lonely People: The Atomized Generation." It provides a helpful look into our growing division just before COVID-19 shut the world down—further distancing society:

> I frequently hear that we are in a crisis of loneliness. . . . It is not simply that people feel lonely; it is that people are less connected than they have ever been. We are in a crisis of atomization. Where loneliness is a feeling inside of us, atomization speaks to the reality of our circumstances. Although loneliness can present itself in any culture and time, its current excess is a byproduct of atomization.
>
> Atomization is the process by which larger units—compounds or cultures, molecules, or families—are broken down into their subcomponents, their individuality gaining clarity as their relationships disintegrate. It affects not just our situation but our capacities. Culturally, we lack the social technology which once would have bound us together. We are atomized in that our lives are less intertwined, but also in that we are less able to withstand close contact and the constraints it brings—this is seen in a breakdown of both romantic relationships as well as friendships.

Now, several years into COVID, it's abundantly clear the pandemic and our attempts to mitigate its impact have only exacerbated our atomization. Reflecting on recent changes, some parents' first thoughts may go to all the academic damage their children suffered in the virus's wake. However, the social damage is just as severe, if not more so.

Writing for *Verywell Family*, author Sherri Gordon explains: "Living through a pandemic has reshaped our kids' friendships in unprecedented ways. Kids were forced to stay apart from their peers because of social distancing requirements, which caused many of them to feel alone, isolated, and bored. Life in lockdown was extremely challenging for kids especially because their social lives were completely disrupted."

Gordon notes that children are more vulnerable to disruption than adults when their routines are drastically altered, especially if the interruption cuts them off from friends and support networks. Which is exactly what happened in the 2020s. Unlike Doris, who experienced her own share of misery—but among friends and loved ones—today's modern youth were put into a shattering form of solitary confinement, albeit one that still enabled them to stream movies and FaceTime. In essence, atomized kids—ones who were *already* growing up on screens—were further distanced from each other, marring their social development. Forget about 4H hayrides. They were told they couldn't see their friends, much less play with them as they used to. Or physically commiserate.

During our own "Great Depression"—this one emotional, but not (yet) financial—youth didn't have release valves. At a time when they most needed social bonding, they couldn't meaningfully connect with their neighbors, classmates, or friends as Doris once did. Gordon further explains that in past studies on children who were isolated due to a disease such as cancer, they struggled to develop meaningful friendships, a problem we're likely to witness with today's youth who were affected by COVID-19 and lockdowns.

Of course, desperate times call for desperate measures as the
saying goes. During the pandemic, concerned experts scrambled
to find safe ways to continue children's education. Many thought
the answer was remote learning. It proved to be nothing short of
a disaster. Fourth-grade teacher Lelac Almagor explained this in
an essay titled: "I Taught Online School This Year. It Was a
Disgrace." Published by *The New York Times* on June 16, 2021,
Almagor describes her experience with online learning on a
typical day:

> Home alone with younger siblings or cousins, kids
> struggled to focus while bouncing a fussy toddler or
> getting whacked repeatedly on the head with a foam
> sword. Others lay in bed and played video games or
> watched TV. Many times each day, I carefully repeated
> the instructions for a floundering student, only to have
> them reply, helplessly, "I'm sorry, I can't hear you," their
> audio squealing and video freezing as they spoke.
>
> Even under optimal conditions, virtual school
> meant flattening the collaborative magic of the class-
> room into little more than an instructional video.
> Stripped of classroom discussion, human connection,
> art materials, classroom libraries, time and space to
> play, virtual school was not school; it was busywork
> obscuring the "rubber-rooming" of the entire
> school system.

THE ROT GOES DEEPER

It will likely take years to even understand the depths of the
atomization of youth culture caused by COVID lockdowns,
let alone reverse the damage. At the same time, it's critical to note
this serious problem wasn't limited to just young people. In fact,
this same harmful atomization has also been rampant in the

workplace. The shift to remote work has wiped out many opportunities to build deep connections with coworkers we once took for granted. Practically overnight, water cooler culture disappeared. Like the proverbial breakroom, physical spaces once existed for coworkers to unite, often discussing their kids or a favorite TV show. A critical component of soft networking, it went away and still hasn't returned completely in most organizations. Sure, you can private message a friend to check in, but can an electronic message ever replace even a brief in-person meeting of the minds?

Although the loss of physical comradery is a serious hit to building connections in the workplace, the problem of atomization goes deeper. Sharon Perley Masling, director of workplace culture consulting at law firm Morgan Lewis, explained to CBS: "The goal is for companies to think practically about how to keep employees socially distant from one another by using signage, blocking off spaces where they would normally congregate and by removing high-touch items. It marks a fundamental shift in how employees would normally interact in an office setting." Employers apparently believed (like schools) that they could replace the bonds employees make with each other via technology and remote work. However, just as this approach failed in schools, it failed in organizations, resulting in workers who felt just as starved for connection as their kids at home playing Fortnite in their pajamas.

Societal atomization and the separation of individuals at the hands of technology and COVID lockdowns is not just a societal nightmare. It's a recipe for disaster in respect to fostering a culture of generosity. Two books provide insight into this phenomenon, explaining *why* we require social cohesion to be successful and how it's been faltering for decades. Way before *Childhood 2.0*.

WE'RE LOOKING FOR OUR TRIBE, BUT OFTEN BOWLING ALONE

In 2014, marketing expert Seth Godin published *Tribes: We Need You to Lead Us* about the need to feel connected to a group. "A tribe is a group of people connected to one another, connected to a leader, and connected to an idea," he wrote. "For millions of years, human beings have been part of one tribe or another." For much of the 20th century, nonprofits like 4-H provided group cohesion. Similar to Elks lodges, Rotary Clubs, or parishes, they functioned as hubs for social and community interaction. Doris's experience in finding connections with a group of peers and eventually her husband is a *real phenomenon*. It's how nonprofits once served as an indispensable part of our social fabric, building and fostering lifelong relationships with avid supporters.

Unfortunately, this tradition of shared connection began eroding in past decades. Political scientist Robert D. Putnam's *Bowling Alone: The Collapse and Revival of American Community* surveys the decline of civic participation, beginning around 1950. Cataloguing declining membership in groups from the Knights of Columbus to the League of Women Voters, to the number of people who volunteer or donate blood, Putnam describes how in-person social intercourse was once as indispensable as today's Wi-Fi. "Americans are right that the bonds of our communities have withered, and we are right to fear that this transformation has very real costs."

THE UNITED STATES OF SCREENS

Perhaps the most alarming thing about *Bowling Alone* is not the profound atomization it describes, but rather, the year it was written: 2001. Published nearly 20 years before the COVID-19 pandemic, it presaged a world of diminished societal bonds—way before lockdowns and distance learning. For years, restaurants and ballparks, once places of rich social interactions, had been emptying, especially as more consumers switched to online shopping.

Back in 2014 reporter David Uberti described the death of the mall for *The Guardian* as a one-time symbol of suburban community life. "For mid-century Americans, these gleaming marketplaces provided an almost utopian alternative to the urban commercial district, an artificial downtown with less crime and fewer vermin. As Joan Didion wrote in 1979, malls became 'cities in which no one lives but everyone consumes.'"

Not long ago, films such as *Mallrats* (1995) and *Fast Times at Ridgemont High* (1982) also depicted malls as desirable hangouts for young people. But that was a different era—before smartphones changed the behavior of a generation. And the generations to come. In a 2017 piece for *The Atlantic*, Jean M. Twenge decries the breakdown of in-person community once so prevalent among youngsters. "Even driving, a symbol of adolescent freedom inscribed in American popular culture, from *Rebel Without a Cause* to *Ferris Bueller's Day Off*, has lost its appeal for today's teens. Nearly all Boomer high-school students had their driver's license by the spring of their senior year; more than one in four teens today still lack one at the end of high school."

Again, this was *before* COVID-19 lockdowns shut down schools and businesses, relegating daily life to screen interactions. Now let's extrapolate to the Generosity Crisis. How did the pandemic affect nonprofit fundraising? Beyond donations already being down from increased social fragmentation and a shift toward online consumerist activities, nonprofits faced a starker challenge yet: how to induce and keep deep connections despite physical distancing? Unfortunately, many nonprofits weren't prepared to answer this in 2020. Worse, they had already seen their donations plummet in recent years because they hadn't innovated ways to better foster tribalistic bonds. As Associated Press first reported in March 2021, "More than one-third of U.S. nonprofits are in jeopardy of closing within two years because of the financial harm inflicted by the viral pandemic."

PROBLEMS WITHIN PROBLEMS

The atomization of US society is compounded by the reduction of our attention spans. We have known for decades that repeated interruptions negatively affect concentration. Dr. Glenn Wilson of the London Institute of Psychiatry researched the impact of persistent interruptions in the workplace. It should come as no surprise that employees distracted by repeated phone calls and emails do their jobs poorly. Just how poorly was the real kicker. Respondents suffered a 10-point drop on their IQ test performance, a greater impact than smoking marijuana. And to put the problem of interruptions into greater relief, more than half of the 1,100 participants admitted stopping work to respond to emails immediately, while almost a quarter confessed to interrupting in-person meetings to reply to communications.

Now, if you think these findings are startling, consider when the research was completed—almost 20 years ago as of this writing. In 2005, *The Guardian* covered Dr. Wilson's research with a headline that seems quaint by today's standards: "Emails 'Pose a Threat to IQ.'" In our current digital society, email is *the least of our interruption problems*. The typical American will receive on their smartphone (near their side 24 hours a day) notifications from multiple social media platforms eager to divert their attention, text messages, reminders from apps, and all manner of video and audio communications. If the arrival of an email knocks 10 points off workers' IQs, imagine what the digital onslaught of Facebook, Twitter, YouTube, and TikTok can do.

CORPORATE AMERICA AND THE ATTENTION ECONOMY

As discussed, some of the biggest corporations dominating the Fortune 100 leverage their insights into consumer behavior—in the form of big data.

Like it or not, many of these companies leverage our lack of attention and atomization. To them, the same threats to non-profits are seen as *monetizable business opportunities for personalization.* The biggest tech companies now gather an obscene amount of intel about every aspect of our lives. This information provides them with an understanding of how to manipulate consumers that's unrivaled in human history. The attention economy is alive and well, built on the backbone of observing and tracking people's behavior. Savvy social media companies have figured out how to gain the best market share—and their strategy isn't pretty (to say it kindly).

Platforms such as Facebook and Twitter live and die by engagement. The longer that users are engaged somewhere digitally, allowing their data to be collected while viewing ads, the richer the tech oligarchs become. So, how *do* you engage people for longer amounts of time? Simple: keep them mad. In the fight for more consumer attention, the tech giants determined that the more people feel outrage and fight with each other, the longer they will spend active with a platform.

In short, social media companies turn misery into money.

U.S. News & World Report documented this disturbing business practice in an August 16, 2021, article titled "Online & Outraged? Facebook 'Likes' Stoke the Fire." The article documents research by psychologists at Yale University who found social media's rewards, including "likes" and "shares," fueldivisive expressions of outrage and even hatred. This is because those who post them receive positive feedback of witnessing others agree with them and spreading their message to a wider audience. As Yale research William Brady explains, "This is the first evidence that some people learn to express more outrage over time because they are rewarded by the basic design of social media."

Make no mistake; this isn't a social media bug. It's a design feature. We know for a fact that the tech companies are aware of the damage their platforms cause. We can thank *The Wall Street Journal* for the scoop. The media outlet published a treasure trove of internal research reports, employee communications, and presentations made to senior management in a series of articles titled "The Facebook Files." The revelations published by the *Journal* are astonishing even to fierce critics of the company. For example, Facebook's own research shows that one in eight users report compulsive use of the company's platforms (which include Instagram and WhatsApp) affects their careers, parenting, and relationships.

FALLOUT

This is the atomization of attention writ large. Worse yet is what Facebook and Instagram do to teen girls. According to Facebook researchers, "Comparisons on Instagram can change how young women view and describe themselves." Problematically, when peer pressure and social media culture convince teenage girls that their tribe should be professional models whose pictures feature heavy filtering and digital observation, they become a ticking time bomb of psychological issues.

Consider Facebook's *own research* into this, as reported by *The Wall Street Journal*:

> "We make body image issues worse for one in three teen girls," said one slide from 2019, summarizing research about teen girls who experience the issues."
> "Teens blame Instagram for increases in the rate of anxiety and depression," said another slide. "This reaction was unprompted and consistent across all groups. Among teens who reported suicidal thoughts, 13% of British users and 6% of American users traced the desire to kill themselves to Instagram, one presentation showed."

Incredibly, despite knowing how bad Instagram and by extension, *all* social media is for teens, the company was developing an "Instagram for Kids" aimed at children between 10 and 12 until popular outcry and governmental inquiries caused them to "pause" development. Instagram head Adam Mosseri said, "Critics of 'Instagram Kids' will see this as an acknowledgment that the project is a bad idea. That's not the case. The reality is that kids are already online, and we believe that developing age-appropriate experiences designed specifically for them is far better for parents than where we are today." Kids may be online, but it should be clear that increased levels of suicide and depression are natural outcomes of a society come unglued by atomization supercharged by a rush toward more screens, not less.

NONPROFITS REMAIN UNSPARED

Americans feeling separated from each other, isolated, and inflamed by social media are major contributors to the dire cultural zeitgeist. Such negative feelings are also directly tied to the distrust in organizations and institutions, whether they be governments, nonprofits, churches, or any other entity suffering a trust deficit today. Yes, according to Edelman's data, corporations are winning the trust war, but that doesn't mean most people are willing to trust *any* person or group these days. People don't even seem willing to trust their own families—look up any famous clan on social media and there's a good chance you will find its loved ones sniping at each other to the great amusement of their fans.

This is horrible for nonprofits. Why? At the root of philanthropy, one doesn't find money, but rather, relationships. How can a society that's become atomized, fearful, distracted by the dopamine hits of social media, and distrustful of everyone around them ever hope to create and sustain those deep relationships needed for generosity to persist in the 21st century? This may seem like an impossible mission, but it's not. There's light at the end of the tunnel in the form of Radical Connection, which we will soon discuss. But first we can learn one more thing from corporate America.

HOW CORPORATIONS OVERCAME ATOMIZATION

As we've documented in previous chapters, for-profit companies have outdone nonprofits in many ways, not only becoming more trusted but also aligning themselves with virtuous missions, visions, and values statements. These companies used another technique to overcome atomization that's left nonprofits in the dust—personalization. Savvy businesses long ago ditched the one-size-fits-all approach, beginning with marketing. Automaker mogul Henry Ford once famously said of his successful Model T, "Any customer can have a car painted any color that he wants so long as it is black." Such a limiting sentiment is entirely foreign to the modern era of corporate marketing. Companies relentlessly personalize offerings to consumers, again capitalizing on big data for their intel.

The level of personalization has reached dizzying heights. *Forbes* collected what it considers to be the 20 most compelling examples from corporate America in a March 2021 article. Consider Gatorade. It has developed a product to analyze a consumer's sweat and provide personalized suggestions on what products suit the user best. In another example, Vail Resorts created an app to track its customers' activity. This data is used to create personalized ski condition reports focusing on the interests of the user instead of the overall condition of the slopes.

For their part, winning corporations are quick to brag about what personalization can do for business. Marketing platform Marketo, owned by software giant Adobe, shares stats about personalization's growing importance. "In one study, 74% of users reported feelings of frustration when website content was not personalized. Another concluded that personalized email marketing has the potential to generate an average ROI of 122%." Marketo further explains personalization has several major benefits to corporations, but the greatest of all is a *better connection with customers*. The company explains: "The average person will see around 1,700 advertisements each month. Your message must cut through the noise—not by being louder, but by being more relevant. For instance, with personalized emails that incorporate your leads' names and other tailored additions, you can see 29% higher unique open rates and 41% higher unique click rates."

Of course, better connection to customers also results in improved revenues, thanks again to personalization. Again, as Marketo writes: "Personalized shopping experiences encourage consumers to become repeat buyers, and brands that create personalized experiences see a spike in transactional rates, buyer retention, and revenue per transaction. It also shows up in their bottom line: personalized marketing can boost revenue by up to 15%. And on the contrary, a lack of personalization can damage your brand: 63% of consumers are highly annoyed when brands rely on old-fashioned, generic ad messaging."

RADICAL CONNECTION IS THE ANSWER

Again, corporate America usurped nonprofits as today's most trusted organizations in part by taking a page from the nonprofit playbook: being centered on a mission or purpose that resonates with the public. If we ever hope to rebuild trust in nonprofits and recreate a *lasting* culture of generosity well into the future, we must take a page back from the corporate playbook.

We must embrace personalization as a pathway to fostering relationships, the first step toward a Radical Connection. Consumers have clearly come to expect on this from every company and organization they interact with, and nonprofits are no exception.

The answer to this crisis may be found in Doris and her friends' deep experiences of connection decades ago. Today's nonprofits must similarly build deep bonds and lasting deep relationships through authentic personalization in a process we dub Radical Connection, which combines the best aspects of the old and the new. The old in this case is the traditional model of philanthropy. Organizations devoted to a mission and operating with strong ethics and transparency work as well as they always have. We're not out to fix them. But that traditional methodology can be *paired* with the personalized, data-driven approach of corporate America to create personalization that isn't just a marketing gimmick—it's instead the result of strong emotional connections between an individual and a nonprofit. This Radical Connection is enduring, unwavering, and often results in the donor becoming an evangelist in partnership with a nonprofit mission.

In many ways, we are talking about a renaissance of agape love, a benevolent feeling toward humankind. Social scientist and author Arthur C. Brooks put it succinctly in an opinion column for the *Washington Post:* "The US is in a crisis of love." We absolutely agree, and what we've documented in this chapter demonstrates just how deep this crisis goes. But the answer is also staring at us straight in the face. The very definition of philanthropy is "the love of humankind." If this is true, if we are indeed suffering a crisis of love, then we have the antidote for our crisis already—it's connection-centric philanthropy. Our mission then is to apply philanthropy in the most effective manner possible, meaning Radical Connection.

SHIFTING FROM THE TRANSACTIONAL TO THE RELATIONAL

For generosity to endure and nonprofits to be successful well into the 21st century, we must leave behind models of transactional connection to our communities and embrace relational Radical Connections. Before we can focus on *how* to do this (as we will in the coming chapters) we must first define the practical *differences* between these two approaches.

To begin, consider the following as a connection scorecard:

Transactional Connection	Radical Connection
Surface level	Deep connection
Mere preference	Love something
Do as little as possible	Go out of your way (to make it happen)
Mention in passing	Share with everyone you know
Second-degree affiliation	Primary affiliation/part of your identity
Forms an opinion	Fosters a visceral reaction
It's nice when you have it	Crave it; miss when you don't have it
Can take it or leave it	Would sacrifice to get it
Neutral	Brings joy, meaning, purpose
Happens one time then forgotten	Happens one time; stays with you forever
Something you did once	Something becomes part of your legacy
I know them or they know me	When I know them *and* they know me

As we know, transactional relationships result in surface-level connections, such as paying the monthly fee for a child's membership to a sports program. Radical Connection, however, results in a deeper connection, such as buying spirit wear for your child's team and putting a sticker on the back of your mini-van to signify your solidarity with your tribe.

Here's another example. Transactional relationships result in *preferences*, such as your desire to attend a performance at a playhouse during matinee hours to receive a discount on price.

Conversely, Radical Connection results in such deep love for an organization that devoted fans will go out of their way to watch a show at any time day or night. A perfect example of this is coauthor Brian's Radical Connection with Pearl Jam, the legendary rock band he has seen more than 50 times (at the time of this book's publishing).

Accordingly, a charitable model based on transactions inspires people to do as little as possible, like clicking a button on a website to donate $5 to a cause. Radical Connection instead inspires people to go out of their way to further an organization's mission, such as volunteering or physically dropping off a donation (and needed supplies) to the organization's headquarters. Or flying halfway around the world to collaborate in a group's efforts. Likewise, a consumer or donor involved in a transactional relationship with your organization may mention you in passing—*if* the topic arises. But individuals who are radically connected to your organization will go out of their way to tell everyone they know about your nonprofit and its latest news. On their own. They are far more engaged than any social media post could hope to be.

Here's yet another distinction. At best, transactional relationships create what are second-degree affiliations. People will consider their primary affiliation to be to a cause like environmentalism. By extension, they may have a second-degree affiliation to an organization they happen to donate to. But Radical Connection *always* creates a primary affiliation—an organization and its mission become an indelible part of the person's identity. Tellingly, mission statements, updates, and advertising tend to have little impact on individuals in a transactional relationship. At best, these materials cause a person to form opinions, such as "This hospital helping children fight cancer is a good thing." Radical Connection fosters a visceral reaction to such materials.

A radically connected individual will be moved to tears over the same update about a hospital's new pediatric cancer program.

There's a legacy component to our discussion. Transactional thinking creates a sense of positivity but only in the *moment*. At the time of the transaction, the individual feels good about what they just did and about themselves. Radical Connection, by its nature, results in the individual focusing on the relationship *constantly*, not just at the moment of transaction. They crave interaction with the group and miss it when it isn't available. They also seek ongoing updates.

One of the greatest drawbacks to a transactional relationship is that it fosters a sense of "I can take it or leave it." In other words, the transaction occurs when it is convenient. When a person feels Radical Connection instead, they will go so far as to sacrifice to achieve the goal they desire. For example, skipping their afternoon Starbucks trip to help someone in need of a meal or a warm touch. Transactional connections also tend to be neutral. It doesn't feel wonderful to participate in a transaction. It's something we must do, another task. Radical Connection defies this feeling. It replaces it with joy, a sense of purpose, and/or an overpowering sense of being on mission. No one remembers a transaction a month later, but Radical Connections create strong memories and a shared sense of values.

In the same vein, a transactional connection happens one time and is then forgotten, whereas a Radical Connection happens one time and creates a lasting impression. Radical Connection is a two-way street, a culmination of a series of events, activities, and impressions. One of the authors has such a memory of donating collected change to a charity drive as a small child. He was too young to understand the concept of nonprofits, but he knew there were children living without all the advantages he had, and he could help them with money he had saved. This memory has lasted decades, another sure sign of Radical Connection.

One of the other key concepts of Radical Connection is its two-way nature. In a transactional relationship, either we know the organization, or they know us. A nonprofit focused on transactions typically knows only its top donors, whereas the entire community knows the organization. (For an example of an organization that knows people without people knowing them, look no further than the IRS.) Yet when Radical Connection is built, we know the organization *and* it knows us. This type of relationship is far more powerful and enduring than any transactional relationship could ever hope to be.

Last, as we know, people give to people. It's an enduring law of philanthropy. And it's an indicator you've achieved Radical Connection when in place of another person, you feel this visceral connection to a nonprofit entity and its brand, mission, or cause. Over the past several decades, we've seen evidence of the Generosity Crisis because too many nonprofit organizations forgot this age-old truth. Instead they have traded the opportunity to build a lasting relationship with a supporter for a shorter-term financial transaction.

Now that we have explored the problems underlying our crisis, it's time to move to Section II: Solutions. In our first chapter, we will describe how nonprofit organizations can achieve Radical Connection with their community through . . . technology? Yes, indeed. We will now learn how to decode generosity.

PART II

OUR SOLUTION

CHAPTER 6

Decoding Generosity

The Procter & Gamble Company is an old-fashioned US manufacturing powerhouse. P&G sold $76 billion worth of consumer goods in 2021, ranging from toothpaste and diapers to laundry detergent and shampoo. If you're one of the few Americans who don't have a house filled with P&G products, just journey down to the grocery store—you practically can't take a step without running into one of their well-known brands. In 2005 P&G acquired another brand to shore up its grooming category. That acquisition hasn't gone as planned.

THE SHAVING SHELLACKING

The company P&G added to its portfolio that year was Gillette, the world leader in shaving products. P&G paid about $57 billion to acquire Gillette *and* its century of customer loyalty and market dominance. For the first few years, the purchase seemed to pay off. Gillette's razors and personal care products generated high margin returns for its new corporate parent.

But the celebrations were not long-lived.

P&G was about to go through tough times. For one thing, shaving habits changed in the 2010s. More men began donning beards as they came back into fashion. Even those who didn't often preferred a scruffy look, meaning that especially young men were shaving less often and thereby buying fewer razors, cans of shaving cream, and related products. But new facial hair trends weren't the biggest hazard P&G ran into with Gillette. They were blindsided by the rise of low-cost internet offerings that upended the industry. Companies such as Dollar Shave Club and Harry's offered web-based subscription models appealing to young people who do their shopping online and were marketed with subversive advertising taking direct aim at traditional razor companies like Gillette.

After P&G caught on to the fact these upstarts were eating its lunch, the consumer goods giant had to act defensively. It increased spending on product innovation and marketing to counter the new narrative, hurting profitability. The fight became even more serious when P&G rival Unilever, which also owns Ben & Jerry's, bought out Dollar Shave Club. Suddenly and dramatically, the Gillette acquisition had reversed course. To this day, P&G continues to battle for market share against its online rivals. In fact, it now offers its own subscription model to regain lost revenue. But in large part, the damage to the brand has already been done. In 2019, P&G took a whopping $8 billion write-down on the value of the Gillette business, with the company's CFO blaming "new competitors" that "entered at prices below the category average" for the massive blow to company earnings.

The average person might be wondering what this has to do with nonprofits. Everything. As described, P&G found itself in a situation many nonprofits similarly face. Unprecedented competition and changing consumer behaviors have taken many by surprise. Likewise, nonprofit leaders are fighting for hearts and wallets against a new generation of savvy companies suddenly talking about their own ethics and missions. This is not a clash whose winner will be decided by financial metrics. It's instead a *competition for connection*. For nonprofits to survive, let alone thrive, in a declining generosity market, they must understand they are in a battle for connection—which P&G realized too late—and take needed steps to understand and build relationships to fuel their ongoing missions.

ARISTOTLE RAISED QUESTIONS WE CAN NOW ANSWER

In case you believe challenges around giving are new, it's worth considering the words of a Greek philosopher taught by Plato. Aristotle wrote about generosity more than 2,300 years ago during the classical period of ancient Greece. He described a problem that has much in common with our Generosity Crisis today: "To give away money is an easy matter, and in any man's power. But to decide to whom to give it, and how large and when, and for what purpose and how, is neither in every man's power—nor an easy matter. Hence, it is that such excellence is rare, praiseworthy, and noble."

Aristotle is pointing out that practically anyone can give money to an organization or a cause. It's now easier than ever, thanks to web-based donation options. Yet what remains difficult is being an *effective philanthropist*—knowing your money will be put to good use, following along with the organization's efforts, and participating in its success. Let it be said, such true philanthropy, which Aristotle labels "rare, praiseworthy, and noble," does not occur due to governmental tax breaks or to follow some asset management strategy. Rather, it happens when a deep visceral connection is established between an individual and a nonprofit mission.

DEMYSTIFYING GIVING

Thanks to innovations unfathomable just several generations ago (let alone in Aristotle's day) we can, for the first time ever, decode generosity. Cutting-edge technology such as deep learning helps us to harness big data, thereby reverse-engineering the reasons people give to nonprofits.

Critically, this tool and others employing AI technology can remove personal biases from the equation—they enable us to discern why people give, not why we *think* people give. What such analysis also consistently proves is our Radical Connection thesis: Donors are driven by depth of connection, identification with a nonprofit, sustained engagement, and alignment of values.

More on AI and big data in a moment. For now, despite the obvious value of gaining an unparalleled understanding of what factors drive giving, some nonprofit leaders recoil from the idea of using tech to humanitarian ends. Why? Perhaps it feels too close to how the for-profit economy operates. Our advice? Sit up and take notice of consumer psychology. It will pay off.

CHANGING MINDS REQUIRED

Nonprofits tend to think of themselves as operating in a different world, separate from for-profit corporations. Yet any demarcating lines that once existed between the two sides have become blurred. The rise of philanthrocapitalism, which takes its approach to business from nonprofits, demonstrates there are no longer two different paradigms. Rather, nonprofits now swim in the same pond as the corporations, and the rules of consumer psychology apply to them in the same way they matter to for-profit enterprises.

What consumer psychology also tells us is that consumers now demand efficient communications personalized to them. Thanks to the likes of Amazon, which delivers real-time precision recommendations for purchases, and Netflix, which suggests specific movies based on thousands of data points, most of us are quite used to big data, even if we don't use the term to describe what's happening. After all, its machinations touch our lives daily. When companies (and especially nonprofits) fail to leverage vast information streams to provide a more personalized level of service, we quickly become dissatisfied. Therefore, nonprofits must leverage such tools to better understand their donors and community in part because *their donors and community have come to expect it.*

Decoding generosity using technology now becomes ever more critical to empower nonprofits into the future. But this knowledge is useless by itself. It must be put to use in practical applications. In Chapter 5 we introduced the key to achieving Radical Connection at scale. Now, it's time to explore that concept at a deeper level.

RADICAL CONNECTION CAN MOVE MOUNTAINS

Introducing . . . the promised land for nonprofits. The antithesis of superficiality, Radical Connection is a bond that can last a lifetime—unless true disaster strikes. It is a visceral understanding between an individual and an organization transcending human explanation. When you are radically connected to an entity, you often can't explain exactly why you feel so strongly about it, but you know with every fiber of your being that it's doing the right things to make the world a better place, as assuredly as you know the sun will rise in the east tomorrow morning. So much so, that you're willing to part with your hard-earned dollars to help further a mission.

Radical Connection also combines surface-level knowledge and rational thinking with an emotional bond that goes beyond simple explanation, yet, when achieved, makes the implausible completely possible. If you think of the special donors and community members who will seemingly move mountains for your nonprofit, you are thinking of radically connected individuals. These kinds of meaningful relationships may seem like aberrations, but they are not. By our nature, individuals desperately hope to form this type of connection with organizations—you just have to find them.

Of course, it can be difficult to fully understand the depth and power of a Radical Connection just from a definition. To provide more clarity, let's consider an example of Radical Connection from the lives of each author.

"The Professional Volunteer"

In 2020, coauthor Nathan read a *New York Times* feature titled "We Had to Do Something" about a group of college students who were deeply concerned about food waste, especially when many families struggle with food security. Published two months into the pandemic, the article revealed a massive social problem for a nation already reeling from a devastating health crisis. "The closure of restaurants, hotels and school cafeterias wiped out huge sources of demand for fresh food, leaving farmers with millions of pounds of excess," explained writers Michael Corkery and David Yaffe-Bellany. "While increased sales at grocery stores have made up for some of that, not since the Great Depression has so much fresh food been destroyed."

Enterprising college students from different universities swooped in to fill this pressing need. They soon connected farmers with food banks, for instance, diverting 50,000 onions destined for destruction on an Oregon farm to Los Angeles, where they were sent to grateful food banks. Likewise, the students bought 10,000 eggs from a California farm, delivering them in a truck to another major food bank.

Nathan read about this organization with growing wonder. The father of two college-aged boys, he very much knows the temptation for (young) people to see a problem and think that it's someone else's concern. The Farmlink Project did not take that view. Instead, its proactiveness struck a chord with Nathan.

In a word, it gave him hope.

Nathan knew he needed to get involved in a meaningful way. His wife's family are third-generation farmers in North Dakota. Firsthand, he has seen how hard the work is, and the pride farmers take in their crops and their lifestyle. They spend day and night nurturing crops so people can benefit from such sustenance. His heart went out to them and other farmers facing the prospect of their efforts being destroyed before ever reaching the public.

Right away, Nathan reached out to Farmlink via email to ask how he could pitch in. From the get-go, Nathan and Farmlink realized there was an instant connect. Like the college students, Nathan shared a passion to do this work. At the same time, Farmlink needed advice on how to run and grow a nonprofit business. After all, it was only launched the previous month by students James Kanoff from Stanford and Aidan Reilly at Brown.

In no time, Nathan and the group began meeting weekly to discuss the ins and outs of the nonprofit business. "As Farmlink grew, so did my engagement," says Nathan. "From weekly calls to hosting a strategic planning retreat where we discussed mission, vision, values I quickly came to see Farmlink represents the future of nonprofit organizations."

Nathan assisted Farmlink in other critical ways. His team at DonorSearch Ai chipped in to help, not only by donating to the cause but also by providing various levels of support, including writing case studies about the fledgling group. DonorSearch also provided Farmlink with data and AI modeling at no charge. Encouraged by Nathan's affinity for the group, his sons flew into action. Toby, a computer scientist, donated much of his time building custom models, visualizing data, and providing insights. His other son, Tate, a college student studying fashion merchandising, screen-printed recyclable tote bags so Farmlink could provide donors a gift of gratitude for making a monthly donation.

Farmlink soon hit its stride. It became an independent 501(c)(3) nonprofit in 2021; Farmlink began with a fiscal sponsor that gave it the ability to receive donations. In the first two years of its existence, it has raised more money and done more good than many nonprofits have in their lifetimes.

Just consider these statistics:

- 70,000,000 total pounds of food rescued
- $4,100,000 + economic relief to farmers and truckers
- 48 states served across 266 underserved communities
- $12,700,000+ fundraised from individual donors as well as corporate and foundation grants

Farmlink's achievements earned it public accolades. The founders appeared on The *Ellen DeGeneres* Show and *Good Morning America*. They have also been awarded the Citizen Honors Service Award and are regularly quoted in the press. For Nathan, this is more than fitting for such a dedicated and innovative organization. "Clearly, my work with Farmlink has become a family affair and a deep passion. These days, I find myself talking about Farmlink to anyone who will listen. It's not just a charity to me, it's now part of my *identity* and an identify that I couldn't be prouder of." He's also quick to add, "While Farmlink is always so respectful and appreciative of my time, I know that between the two of us, *I* get more out of this relationship."

"A Chaminade Man"

Coauthor Brian has a Radical Connection with an educational institution, the high school he graduated from, Chaminade High School in Long Island, New York. A Catholic school with roughly 1,700 students, it's renowned for producing young men that become both leaders and gentlemen. The school is a core part of Brian's identity, as well as that of his brothers and brothers-in-law, who also went there. As Brian explains, "I can see how someone carries themself and guess they went to Chaminade." Recognizing a Chaminade man isn't even dependent on a telltale Long Island accent because the school draws students from around the region—it's more about the positive qualities the institution instills in its graduates, including Brian.

In fact, Brian attributes much of his success in life to concepts, skills, and a positive way of being he was introduced to at Chaminade. He expresses this Radical Connection to his high school through not only financial donations but also sharing his time and energy cultivating the next generation of Chaminade men. A key sign of Radical Connection is identifying with the organization's legacy, which Brian does, by socializing with alumni and taking pride in the school's 90-plus-year history.

Another way Radical Connection is strengthened is by external validation, which is certainly Brian's experience with Chaminade. It's common for figures of national stature to speak at university commencements and other events, but certainly less so at high schools. Can you think of a time a government official at the highest levels of power visited a high school they didn't attend for a speech that wasn't associated with a tragedy or a blatant PR event?

Well, it happened at Chaminade.

In 2018, General Peter Pace, former chairman of the Joint Chiefs of Staff, graced Chaminade to share with the students his own Radical Connection to the school—which seems surprising at first glance. Unlike Brian, Pace did not attend the high school. He hadn't even heard of it until he was a commissioned officer in the Vietnam War. As a young Marine Corps 2nd lieutenant serving his first deployment in Vietnam, Pace was struck by the character and integrity displayed by one of his enlisted soldiers, Lance Corporal Guido Farinaro. Farinaro demonstrated the impeccable strength of character expected of officers, while also helping his fellow soldiers and civilians in uncommon, laudable ways.

Duly impressed, Pace made it a point to learn Farinaro's history. Topping the list? His formidable and forming experience attending Chaminade. Although Farinaro was tragically killed in combat months after their meeting, Pace never forgot the extraordinary man who made such an impression on him in their short time together. Pace told this story to an enraptured audience of students and alumni a few years ago, describing his own Radical Connection without, of course, using our specific term.

Yet the meaning was the same. Pace explained to the Chaminade crowd that he has lived all his days in a way he thinks Farinaro would approve of. He even went so far as to write this same Chaminade graduate's name down when he testified before Congress. "No matter how intense the questioning would get, I would look at that piece of paper and say, 'This is your responsibility. You owe it to Guido.'"

Pace would later go on to create a scholarship for Chaminade students in Farinaro's name. His ongoing association with the high school exemplifies Radical Connection. It presents a compelling example of how others who also become radically connected to an organization can reinforce such a strong bond, paying it forward to future generations.

"The Guy Who Never Wins the Raffle Gets Lucky"

Coauthor Michael's example of Radical Connection is also tied to education, but not an institution he attended. His is based on his son's schooling. Children are a common source of Radical Connection—we love our little ones so deeply that when we perceive an organization is providing them a beneficial leap forward, the bond we feel to that group is indelible and visceral.

In Michael's case, the entity is Classical Christian Academy (CCA) near Coeur d'Alene, Idaho. CCA has only been a part of his family's life for a few years, but already it provides a powerful and meaningful Radical Connection. As a former professor and a college essay coach, Michael has observed firsthand the sorry state of today's educational system. "When I first began my company, I coached dozens of juniors and seniors at well-endowed private high schools. Though they all had superb grades on paper, most could not write a 250-word essay on why they should attend their college of choice. More alarmingly, they couldn't even formulate what they wanted to write about due to poor educational preparation."

But CCA is in a league of its own. Committed to teaching in the old-fashioned model that has sustained Western civilization for millennia, it truly prepares students in the Trivium: grammar, logic, and rhetoric. In an era when many young people are functionally illiterate, CCA students are reading classics like *The Brothers Karamazov* and learning to read and write in cursive. The school is also committed to producing young men and women of strong moral character.

From the moment Michael met with headmaster Bill Stutzman and learned of the school's approach, harking back to a more rigorous era of academic excellence, he was hooked. "I got tears in my eyes just hearing about the wonderful education my son would receive—something so drastically different from the way school is unfolding these days." As he explains, his little boy loves his school. He's happy walking into CCA in the morning and seems even happier when his mom picks him up at the end of the day.

Michael's Radical Connection to CCA is demonstrated in several ways, which is typical of radically connected individuals to any organization. He contributes funds beyond tuition to help bridge the gap for underfunded students. He also donates his time to the academy, applying his skills to complimentary video work to help the school save money and produce marketing materials.

But the true test of Michael's Radical Connection came when the self-professed "unluckiest man in the history of lotteries" won big in the CCA raffle.

Similar to many CCA parents, Michael buys tickets for the drawings that contribute to the school's operations, not expecting anything, as he's never won any raffle, giveaway or sweepstake in his life.

All that would change. In 2021, CCA launched its largest annual raffle to date for an amazing grand prize—a shiny new car. Michael bought tickets, telling his wife, "If we win this, we're giving the car back to the school." To his shock, Michael clinched the raffle. The guy who never wins *anything* had suddenly triumphed in a big way. What Michael didn't know was that his Radical Connection to CCA was about to be tested. That deep affinity was easy to express when buying $10 raffle tickets, but harder when a $30,000 vehicle was on the line.

Would self-interest win out over his connection to CCA? It was an easy decision for Michael. He told the school to keep the car. Michael is by no means so wealthy that a new auto would not help his family. Yet his bond to CCA is so meaningful, so *radical*, he knew he had to forgo the grand prize. He didn't lose sleep over the situation, either. The decision turned a positive fundraising event for CCA into a grand slam homerun, deepening Michael's already-strong relationship with his son's school.

RADICAL CONNECTION IN THE CREATOR ECONOMY

If you want to find more examples of Radical Connection not involving nonprofits or massive corporations, consider the creator economy—the fast-growing population of YouTubers, TikTokers, live streamers, and artists who earn a living not by collecting a paycheck from an employer but from supporters and subscribers. (If you don't watch YouTube or streams on Twitch, just find a teen and ask them about their favorite streamer. They're likely able to quote how many views they average and their subscriber numbers, which are public information.)

Tech expert Kevin Kelly published a related essay in *Wired* a few years ago explaining the creator economy and how it's built on Radical Connection with fans:

> To be a successful creator you don't need millions. You don't need millions of dollars or millions of customers, millions of clients or millions of fans. To make a living as a craftsperson, photographer, musician, designer, author, animator, app maker, entrepreneur, or inventor you need only thousands of true fans.
>
> A true fan is defined as a fan that will buy anything you produce. These diehard fans will drive 200 miles to see you sing; they will buy the hardback and paperback and audible versions of your book; they will purchase your next figurine sight unseen; they will pay for the "best-of" DVD version of your free YouTube channel; they will come to your chef's table once a month. If you have roughly a thousand of true fans like this (also known as super fans), you can make a living—if you are content to make a living but not a fortune.

Driving 200 miles from home to attend a Pearl Jam concert or purchasing a rare Japanese pressing of a CD as a memento are behaviors of what Kelly calls "super fans," but we also recognize this as surefire signs of Radical Connection. A bond with both mental and emotional implications, it drives creators to greater levels of success at a time in which data has usurped oil as the world's most valuable commodity. But guess what? The same underlying logic applies to nonprofits. Now for a key caveat.

RADICAL CONNECTION WITH EVERYONE IS IMPOSSIBLE

By now we hope you're revved up about Radical Connection and what it can do for your organization. You've probably even assessed some of your own allegiances, determining if, in fact, they constitute Radical Connections. Inevitably, people who learn about this concept embrace it with gusto. They want to become radically connected with everyone in their community. *It's the best thing since sliced bread. Let's scale it to everyone we can!*

This is where we must pump the breaks, because it is impossible to radically connect to everyone. The art of successfully building Radical Connection is to identify the *right people* in your community who have the potential to achieve this level of affiliation, then investing the significant time, energy, and resources needed to produce indelible bonds. If you do this right, it holds the potential to transform your organization. Forever. As such, your principal efforts should center on working toward this goal. (Even if your pipeline is only 1,000 strong with the potential for Radical Connection, this is now the ambition to work toward. After all, those 1,000 folks will be your strongest evangelists— per Kevin Kelly.)

Importantly, investing in Radical Connection means valuing relationships over any other consideration. Remember, the adage in nonprofits: "people give to people." This phrase is frequently said within nonprofit circles, but rarely changes how nonprofits prioritize their strategies or time. As the authors can attest, the most common response in too many nonprofit meetings is something along the lines of, "What's the next video we are producing to convince people to give?"

In other words, the concentration is on activities to raise funds, or what the team *thinks* will raise funds, forgetting entirely that the emphasis should first be on the connection to others, and once that is authentically achieved, money will follow.

It may sound quaint to phrase it this way in the era of TikTok, but if you are a nonprofit leader, we encourage you to think more like the TV show *Cheers*. Though a work of fiction, the 1980s sitcom evokes a simpler age when friends would congregate at a place where "everybody knows your name." Too many of us live lightning-paced existences now, and yet, the power of tech might just enable us to know each other on the level of friends sipping a cold one. If only we can adjust our thinking.

To draw another analogy from pop culture, consider Tom Cruise's strategy as a sports agent in *Jerry Maguire*. The whole film is really about Radical Connection—though once again, the characters never use that term. Nonprofits, take note: Jerry slogs through a hollow joke of a life as a superficial sports agent fixated on snagging more client endorsements. He's just the guy to say, "What's the next video we are producing?"

It's only when he recommits himself to prioritizing relationships over money and building deeper relationships with fewer clients that he finds real success—and happiness. Nonprofit leaders might consider putting a slightly different spin on this approach by deepening the donor journey. By doing right by those you serve, the superstar "Rod Tidwells" of your community will organically bubble up to the surface. Of course, Jerry had to do it all alone. The task can be made much easier for nonprofits possessing a strong team committed to acting with purpose.

Now that we have explored the macro dynamics of our concept, let's drill down for more specifics.

THE FOUR RULES OF RADICAL CONNECTION

We often take for granted, and grossly underestimate, the power of "connection" in our everyday lives. In its simplest form, we may have a social media connection to someone we've never met. In its most complex form, connection can manifest as a visceral connection of the soul with someone we're introduced to for the first time. When it comes to the altruistic form of generosity, the role of connection cannot be understated. Creating a sustainable increase in generosity requires rethinking our preconceived notions of connection. Whether as a contributor or recipient of charitable intent, understanding and observing the following guidelines will help reset definitions of what meaningful connection looks like in the short term and long term.

Rule 1: Generosity Follows Radical Connection

Radical Connection manifests itself in the form of generosity—not the other way around. In fact, it can *only* happen when money is not the top priority in the relationship. Money creates imbalance in associations. Reducing its importance enables bonds to be built in less biased ways. Patagonia exemplifies this rule. It made a choice to prioritize environmental concerns over sales, and the dollars flowed in. In other words, they decreased the emphasis on sales with their famous, Do Not Buy This Jacket campaign, focusing instead on the alignment of their corporate values, and it paid off for them. In the nonprofit economy, this happens when leaders stop asking major gift officers, "How much money is in your portfolio of prospects?" and instead ask, "How deep are the relationships in your portfolio of prospects?"

Rule 2: Authenticity and Inclusion Are Critical to Success

Radical Connection can only be fostered when mutual respect and a configuration of values exists celebrating diversity of thought and experience. Your organization must consistently embrace people of all walks of life without bias. Only by embracing folks in all their many variations can we grow in unison, especially as we dispense with shallow differences. To witness this philosophy in action, look to the wildly successful hockey coach Herb Brooks, architect of the 1980s "Miracle on Ice" victory over Russia. Brooks's approach to the Olympics was to build a varied team of players who meshed well together—not simply the most talented players at each position. By fostering all-encompassing teamwork and deep bonds, Brooks and his team did the impossible.

Rule 3: Transparency and Accountability Are Indispensable

For Radical Connection to be formed and maintained, nonprofits must do what they say they will with the highest ethical standards. This means fulfilling promises, providing financials, and exposing weaknesses when they occur with integrity and consistency. As we have seen, trying to paper over problems only leads to more problems. Vulnerability, however, evokes trust. Radical Connection is about meeting people where they are without putting up a façade. Transparency and accountability create the "we are in this together" mentality, engendering strong relationships. For instance, Brian has been in donor meetings when transparency was employed to unusual effect. One time a nonprofit leader candidly expressed uncertainty about the organization's ability to hit its fundraising targets and fully fund its mission. Instead of blowing up in his face, this admission opened the door to an honest conversation with the donors in the room who felt respected and appreciated by such candor. Surprisingly (to those unfamiliar with Radical Connection) the donors felt even *more* invested with the organization and were willing to fund its efforts to an even greater degree to ensure its success.

Rule 4: It's About the Organization and Mission—Not You

Radical Connection is about the individual on the donor side, *not* about individuals on the organizational side. It takes proactive and consistent effort to keep focus on the goal at hand and not on your own ego. When leaders put the mission above themselves and especially treat their team as stewards *in service of that mission*, the environment is ripe for Radical Connection. To this point, Nathan performed a study of the 25 top donors at UC San Diego, revealing the average length of time they had been giving to the university was 18 years. During this period, the college averaged a staggering 14 different gift officers— nearly a different one per year. Clearly, the Radical Connection felt by donors was to the university and its mission, and not to any temporary relationship with a transitory gift officer or even senior leaders.

HOW ONE COMPANY BUILDS RADICAL CONNECTIONS

Entrepreneur Bill TeDesco has enjoyed a highly winning career, but not because he did the same thing as everyone else. Defying conventional wisdom, he presaged groundbreaking ways tech companies could use innovation for greater generosity. Bill knew there were better ways to predict future giving than by merely focusing on a person's wealth. He founded DonorSearch in 2007 with the recognition that affinity to a cause and/or mission is a better indicator of generosity than the money in someone's bank account.

Driven by his vision, his company set to work creating the world's foremost database of donor intelligence. (They were leveraging big data for philanthropy before much of the world ever knew this term.) Fast forward 15 years. DonorSearch, of which Nathan leads its AI division, now combines its industry-leading database with advanced technology to determine donor sentiment for leading nonprofits, including universities, hospitals, museums, and multinational organizations. These digital tools measure the depth of affinity individuals feel to an organization using algorithms that continually learn, ever increasing their accuracy.

UNPRECEDENTED PRECISION

Using the most advanced machine learning systems (which until recently had only been accessible to the largest for-profit corporations) vastly improves nonprofits' ability to be spot-on in interactions with potential donors. In fact, the use of AI by the early adopters in the nonprofit sector have moved this body of work beyond its initial hypothesis of predicting generosity and into the data science stage. According to a recent AI in Advancement Advisory Council study, 89% nonprofit professionals believe that AI can make their organization more efficient. Yet the "State of Artificial Intelligence in the Nonprofit Sector" study also concluded that 25% of nonprofits report AI is either deployed in the implementation phase or experimental. (This is compared with 97.2% for private sector organizations.)

Ultimately, with hundreds of algorithms capable of handling a virtually unlimited number of variables, the exact characteristics of givers and non-givers can be calculated with uncanny accuracy.

The net result? A clear road map of what these commonalities are—down to the tenth of a decimal point. The insights provided are astonishing. More to the point, the data shows how repeat donors value their personal relationships with an organization over everything else, especially if they connect with an individual. Although the data on such repeat donors is valuable, precision becomes worth its weight in gold when it can predict first-time donors and their behavior. Studying prospect mentality through the lens of emerging tech is a true lesson in patternmaking. Sophisticated AIs can uncover subtle signals no human can, indicating when someone is about to make their first gift.

One indicator for educational institutions is the number of emails alumni open. "Our model quickly determined for one university that non-donors were most likely to make their first gift when opening alumni newsletters on Tuesdays, Wednesdays, and Thursdays between 2:00 p.m. and 4:00 p.m. local time," Nathan explains. This is just one datapoint out of more than 1,000 that are calculated on an ongoing basis to determine if a person's engagement is increasing or decreasing over time. "This unparalleled precision has the power to usher in a new era of giving where someone's chance of donating can be calculated specifically to an exact organization," he added. Even better, the algorithmic model is transparent, not a black box, where each data point being used can be viewed and interrogated to provide insights on behavior and audited for bias.

UNPRECEDENTED PERSONALIZATION

Clearly, the use of responsible AI is an undeniable boon for philanthropy. As we have stated—and savvy companies know all too well—today's consumers expect messaging to be personalized, delivered in the right way, at the right time, and with the right call to action. And this expectation extends to nonprofits. Whether we like it or not. After all, when nonprofits bungle their outreach, like mistaking a wife for a husband on a form letter, it's a major turnoff. (Remember our fictional couple Tony and Carmen?) Such gaffes make donors think your organization is disorganized and clumsy—or worse, indifferent—setting the stage for the opposite of Radical Connection. Nathan's favorite example of handling personalization correctly is a recent stay at a Ritz-Carlton hotel, where he was enjoying some fresh air on a bench when an employee walked by and said, "Good morning, Mr. Chappell."

Talk about personalization. Technology, especially the cutting-edge work being done by Nathan's team at DonorSearch, allows nonprofits to achieve new levels the market now demands—and many corporations already leverage. Remember, fundraising works best when three factors are aligned:

- **Emotional:** How will this gift make me feel?
- **Rational:** How will this gift make me look to others?
- **Financial:** How will this gift affect my capital?

Radical Connection enables such alignment, and technology allows it to happen faster, more accurately, and with personalization. In our view, Radical Connection is also best cultivated via the combination of these five factors:

- Precision at scale
- Empathy for the community
- Increase in transparency and trust
- Individualization and personalization
- Buy-in with mission/cause

One More Thing: Stop Looking at Companies as the Bad Guys

One of our primary insights thus far is that nonprofits shouldn't look at corporations with suspicion; instead, they should learn from their ability to "unscale" their business practices and apply them to their own fundraising. Done right, the result is an efficient use of tech from corporate America, paired with the passion and purpose of a nonprofit. This can lead to Radical Connection and unprecedented levels of success. Remember, money to fund a mission is the desired end goal. But money is merely the manifestation of generosity, and generosity is the expression of Radical Connection. The world of today is a competition for such affiliation. Every company and nonprofit in the world are no longer just trying to sell something; rather, they are trying to connect with you in a deep, personal way.

At the same time, we must always keep in mind that no relationship is set in stone—it's constantly shifting. Every day, individuals draw closer to or move farther away from every organization. Your view of a for-profit or nonprofit organization changes constantly as you reevaluate your alignment with that entity based on things you see, hear, or experience. Likewise, no person is either a donor or a prospect, but instead an *individual* with the potential for a deeper bond with an organization if it provides the right opportunity to engage based on one's value system.

Naturally, the shifting sands of affiliation are inescapable because humans are flesh and blood creatures guided by emotion over rationality—no matter how much we protest otherwise. Knowing how people's hearts and minds can change is precisely why AI is leveraged to continually monitor behavioral data. People's affiliations can shift in real time, making advances in technology one of the major ways to keep up with this reality.

Leveraging innovation to assess and refine the donor journey in real time is a fundamental shift in fundraising practices. When the ultimate act of personalization is married with precision, it acknowledges that individuals are constantly changing and growing instead of treating them like static beings.

In the next chapter, we'll explore even more how treating people like individuals can pay big dividends to both corporations and nonprofits alike.

CHAPTER 7

When Generosity Is Good
for Business—and Society

Some industries have better reputations than others for embracing the mission-driven philanthrocapitalism mimicking nonprofits—at least in the eyes of the public. Think of clothing companies like TOMS, a trailblazer in marketing its poverty-ending mission. Another example can be found in internet-based apparel company Bombas. It donates clothing to homeless shelters with every purchase. Bombas proudly states it has given out more than 50 million items, primarily socks and underwear, to 3,500 giving partners in all 50 states. "One Purchased = One Donated" is such a central part of the company's value proposition to customers and it features in every advertisement.

Corporate responsibility is also on the rise in the food industry. Ben & Jerry's has inspired a wave of mission-driven corporate responsibility in this sector. Likewise, Panera Bread's more than 2,000 restaurants provide unsold baked goods to local nonprofits daily. The program amounts to more than $100 million in donated food yearly. The Panera Bread Foundation also provides grants to nonprofits focused on mentorship, professional development, and workforce skill building. The company has several other programs designed to assist nonprofits and build mission-driven connection with its customers.

Food and textiles are just a few industries with numerous companies embracing mission-driven philanthrocapitalism. What about finance? Banks and stockbrokers are decidedly *not* the first entities you might think of as being ethical and values-driven. But why not? For one thing, so many negative feelings about the financial sector are reflected in popular culture. Think about how banks are portrayed in films. In older fare, such as *Bonnie and Clyde* (1967), the eponymous antiheroes earn audience empathy in large part because we see that amoral banks are perfectly okay with seizing family farms after a few missed mortgage payments. Stockbrokers don't come across much better. The iconic image of *Wall Street*'s (1987) Gordon Gekko with his slick-backed hair telling us "Greed is good" provokes a near universal image of sleazy cutthroat brokerages in the minds of viewers. Despite their reputation as operating in the nexus of old-fashioned heartless, profit-focused capitalism, coauthor Brian and his consulting firm took on the ultimate challenge—showing one such brokerage how to be mission-driven and embrace social responsibility.

Turning Over a New Leaf at TD Ameritrade

When Brian isn't writing books and articles on maximizing the effectiveness of nonprofits and helping corporations embrace the positives of philanthrocapitalism, he's putting his thought leadership into practice with his consulting company, Changing Our World, Inc. Changing Our World enables nonprofit clients to strengthen their fundraising efforts. It also consults with their for-profit peers on developing corporate social engagement.

Initially, TD Ameritrade approached Brian and his team based on multiple recommendations from both companies and nonprofits that enjoyed success after working in close partnership with Changing Our World. TD Ameritrade's leadership was upfront in their initial meetings—the brokerage powerhouse knew it was falling behind the times and was in desperate need of a formal corporate social responsibility (CSR) plan. In 2016, Brian and his team took on the challenge and got to work. Still, some members of Changing Our World were skeptical at first about their ability to create an effective CSR plan. Despite any initial reservations, a group of Brian's senior impact consultants flew into action.

What you should know is Changing Our World's differentiator is its multistep approach to each engagement. First, the team immerses itself deeply into a client's operations to gain both the big picture and the perspective of day-to-day operations. Next, it uses these data points to inform its decisions, creating signature strategies built to suit each client's unique situation. Finally, Changing Our World consultants work together with clients to implement new policies so that there is no danger of important changes devolving into mere lip service.

At TD Ameritrade, immersion meant sending a team to corporate headquarters in Omaha, Nebraska. The "equality before the law state" is home to seemingly endless farms as well as one of America's most popular stockbrokers. TD Ameritrade was founded there in 1971 and has annual revenues of more than $4 billion. The consultants quickly uncovered a set of challenges as well as positives that would shape their work with the financial firm.

On the challenge side, the company had no formal CSR policy. Instead, it possessed a smattering of confusing and sometimes contradictory responsibility programs within different teams and divisions. Changing Our World quickly determined one of its key tasks was to add structure and consistency to TD Ameritrade's approach to CSR. At the same time, it also enabled the company to measure and articulate the value of progress toward key social impact goals, stakeholder expectations, and business objectives. A major undertaking no doubt, but the consultants were also pleasantly surprised by their findings about TD's strong corporate culture and the winning attitudes among employees at all levels of the financial powerhouse.

Brian's team was happy to learn there were very few (if any) Gordon Gekko clones roaming the halls. Instead of scheming

Wall Street stereotypes as might be expected, Changing Our World found the company to be driven by a unique and very authentic culture of teamwork, inclusion, and personal accountability. TD Ameritrade had also built a strong legacy of grassroots employee engagement over its almost 50 years in business, so it had a solid foundation for adding a formal CSR program.

Based on this deep understanding of the organization and its employees, Changing Our World created a CSR befitting TD Ameritrade's culture and vision. Titled "Creating Pathways to Prosperity," the CSR created in part with Brian's team came to organize how the company brings its purpose to life. That purpose was also formalized in 2017: "to transform lives and investing for the better." TD Ameritrade established its social responsibility efforts toward achieving this goal into three central pillars:

- Confidence

- Culture

- Commitment

The pillars reflect the company's aspirations of being a mission-driven brokerage while also honoring its longstanding employee culture of giving back. Just as important as gaining buy-in for these three pillars from every level of the company, Brian's consulting team established program metrics and key performance indicators (KPIs) to quantitatively measure the impact of its CSR efforts from both corporate and social perspectives.

For a financial firm deeply immersed in the world of price-to-earnings ratios and other stock market performance numbers, the KPIs transformed TD Ameritrade's CSR from well-meaning mumbo-jumbo into trackable, sustainable corporate activities. Despite the success of creating the brokerage's first formal social responsibility framework, it was clear to the company and Changing Our World that there was more to be done. Instead of packing up and leaving Nebraska for the big city, the team dug in to face a new challenge—creating an effective community involvement plan with a combination of the company's three core values of confidence, culture, and commitment.

Changing Our World's next challenge was to create a community engagement platform balancing targeted social impact with the company's tradition of employee-led volunteerism and giving. To accomplish this feat, the consultants held group discussions and interviews to answer the burning question at the heart of the stated mission of transforming investing "for the better": what could TD Ameritrade do to better the world as a stockbroker?

Answers flooded in from all areas of the company, and although their wording and emphasis were sometimes different, the message was loud and clear, not to mention astoundingly consistent from junior customer service reps to the C-suite. En masse, TD Ameritrade employees made it clear to Changing Our World they felt one of the problems with their business was that their clientele were primarily composed of people with high financial literacy and an established level of personal wealth. Also, many of the company's younger customers happened to be the children and grandchildren of existing clientele, who passed such financial knowledge onto them. If the company did truly wish to transform investing for the better, its goal really should be to extend such expertise to the many people who unfortunately don't receive it through family ties—particularly those in low-income and underserved communities. Critically, many employees felt strongly that this goal should extend to *all* ages, from adults to children—just as financial literacy is shared by privileged families.

Inspired by the staff's shared vision of transforming investing for the better by educating disadvantaged populations, the Changing Our World team created an audacious plan to apply TD Ameritrade's core competencies to a brand-new audience. A team of TD consultants, company employees, and representatives from the 4-H nonprofit developed a first-of-its-kind primer based on research into those key skills and behaviors needed to succeed financially. The *Smart Cents Playbook* was designed to enhance financial literacy in adults and children while putting readers on the path to a healthy monetary future.

Still, the team was careful to not inadvertently damage the company's strong tradition of grassroots employee action. To maintain TD Ameritrade's culture of giving back, the team also produced programs to encourage volunteerism and philanthropy instead of making internal stakeholders feel stifled by strict corporate structures. The programs are familiar to some we've mentioned, such as the one from Panera Bread. The brokerage established a community grants endeavor to fund local nonprofits lining up with employees' passions. It also created a "Dollars for Doers" venture to donate cash grants to nonprofits that employees donate time to. Finally, TD set up a matching gifts program to pair financial donations made by workers. All these programs reinforced the existing corporate culture of giving back *and* made staff feel their zeal and interest in giving back was rewarded by TD Ameritrade "joining the team."

INSIGHTS

TD Ameritrade's successful launch of its first-ever CSR as well as the creation of an innovative financial literacy program serves as a wake-up call to every corporation and nonprofit in America. If a midwestern financial powerhouse with little experience in these waters can do CSR right, then no organization has an excuse not to embrace this new business approach (or achieve a nonprofit's mission). In fact, the incredible benefits of powerful and effective CSR from the corporate perspective are best captured in the concept of the triple bottom line. Harvard Business School's *Business Insights Blog* explains how this concept serves as an expansion of focus from the traditional measure of success—*profits*—to also consider CSR measures. As Kelsey Miller explained for Harvard:

> The **triple bottom line** is a business concept that posits firms should commit to measuring their social and environmental impact—in addition to their financial performance—rather than solely focusing on generating profit, or the standard "bottom line." It can be broken down into "three Ps": **profit, people,** and the **planet.** [Emphasis in the original]

Each of the three bottom lines in the sustainable business model possesses its own unique elements, along with how it interacts with the other two bottom lines. Let's investigate each.

Profit

The oldest bottom line is the easiest to understand. It's been the primary focus of the business world for millennia. Companies plan their practices and strategic initiatives on maximizing revenue and minimizing costs. At the same time, they act to lower risk from competition and other external factors.

This was the way of the world in the past, but that's all changing. Mission-driven corporations still emphasize the need for profits, but not at the expense of stakeholders beyond shareholders and management, including not only employees but also the community, the environment, and the world at large.

As we have seen, many companies that take this approach have seen a surprising jump in business success, such as Patagonia and Ben & Jerry's. Certainly, from a nonprofit perspective, the concept of profit can be equated to fundraising toward a goal. Likewise, devoid of fundraising, a nonprofit can suffer from the same plight.

PEOPLE

The second bottom line tends to be confusing. The natural question is "Exactly *which* people do we care about?" For years, legacy capitalism had a very specific group of people they focused on: shareholders and executives. After all, the traditional purpose of a company's existence was once to increase shareholder value.

Philanthrocapitalism and the new breed of mission-driven corporations expands this narrow focus by reexamining their true stakeholders. As noted, stakeholders invariably include shareholders and executives, but they also now extend to include the employee population of a company as well as the community, especially customers and those in geographic proximity to the company and its operations.

Considering all these groups as stakeholders is the key to sustainability. The "people" bottom line certainly played a big role in TD Ameritrade's CSR work. Its educational program is aimed at stakeholders beyond its current customers, and its new policies encourage volunteerism and other contributions by employees to the wider community.

One of the major ways companies interested in improving their people bottom line act is by partnering with nonprofit agencies specializing in a particular area of interest. TD Ameritrade teamed up with 4-H (first mentioned in Chapter 5 in our discussion of *Childhood 2.0*) to connect underserved youth. Likewise, Panera Bread partners with food pantries, and Bombas aids homeless shelters in distributing clothing to those in need. Forward-thinking nonprofits should be receptive to those corporations that view them as the ideal partner to accomplish a shared goal.

PLANET

More companies than ever are responding to their customers' urgent interest in preserving our natural environment. Yes, some companies believe they have little responsibility to help the earth, especially if their model doesn't involve dirty factories spewing pollution and cutting down trees. But that is a narrow view. The Climate Disclosure Project's Carbon Majors Report 2017 claims that 100 energy companies account for 71% of global emissions, but would Google and TD Ameritrade's servers function without the energy these companies provide? Where does the energy to charge Tesla cars come from? With a more expansive perspective suggesting practically everything we do relies on energy production, the planet (rightfully) becomes a shared concern for every company *and* nonprofit.

Of course, the planet bottom line goes far beyond attempting to decrease an organization's carbon footprint. Other popular considerations are ethically sourced materials, cutting down on energy consumption, and changing logistics practices so shipping products affect the environment as little as possible. Although once the province of the largest companies in the world, such initiatives are common in medium and small companies as well, not to mention the many nonprofits engaged in this vital work.

WHY THE TRIPLE BOTTOM LINE MATTERS

Some philanthrocapitalism critics argue mission-driven companies pursue a claim of improving communities and the planet at the expense of profitability. Not true. The triple bottom line is a model demonstrating how revenues needn't suffer while a company tries to improve the world around it. In fact, there is more evidence than ever before that companies can perform well financially while doing good things for stakeholders of all types and the environment. To this point, Harvard Business School professor Rebecca Henderson explains: "In many situations, it's possible to do the right thing and make money at the same time. Indeed, there's good reason to believe that solving the world's problems presents trillions of dollars' worth of economic opportunity."

This is certainly the belief within the halls of TD Ameritrade. Early evidence shows existing customers strongly approve of the company's efforts to provide financial literacy education to underserved communities. Also, most investors welcome additional investors to the market because they understand the stock market is not a zero-sum game. If more investors are busy buying and selling shares of stock, all can potentially benefit via increased volume and liquidity. To these individuals, TD Ameritrade's CSR programs act as a *competitive advantage*. If a stockbroker with similar services and fees tries to win their business, they may recall the positive feelings they have toward TD Ameritrade's initiatives and resist changing brokers.

But this isn't the only potential financial advantage for the company. The brokerage giant understands that its community education program, designed to increase financial literacy in youth and underserved communities, can act as a pipeline for future customers. Young people who gain from the program and begin investing early on are likely to stick with the company that reached out to them *before* they had money to invest, loyally opening TD Ameritrade accounts without ever considering the competition. This is in some respects a similar strategy to Apple's educational strategy—kids who grow up using Macs at school are likely to adopt Apple products when they are of an age to buy a computer for themselves.

These advantages can extend far beyond the world of corporations and into nonprofits as well. Remember, TD Ameritrade partnered with 4-H on the financial literacy project. If participants later become wealthy, especially based on their newfound financial literacy, they are likely to remember the entity that helped them achieve such success. Likewise, when a homeless person who received free clothing from Bombas at a shelter gets back on their feet, they are likely to feel gratitude toward *both* Bombas and the facility that once distributed the free apparel.

Such potential financial successes may nonetheless lead some to cynically suggest these companies are engaging in no more than "cause marketing," designed to pull on consumers' heartstrings and desire to contribute to a better world by buying the right socks or pastries or investing with the right broker. Actually, these companies are leaving cause marketing in the dust, because they've found the power of Radical Connection— that's what is *really* going on when corporations embrace the triple bottom line.

Social Responsibility Forms Radical Connection

Even so, it is a mistake to believe corporations must *all* be mission-driven to achieve Radical Connection. Frequently, this desired affiliation is instead formed by emotions such as nostalgia and positivity built up over time. Most every adult has a product, service, or location eliciting a rush of pleasure based on warm memories. For example, your brand loyalty to Coca-Cola might be based on sharing a cold can of Coke with your grandfather on a summer's day.

However, many, if not most, companies don't have the luxury of Coca-Cola's celebrated history as a business with massive brand loyalty. Instead, they must seize the opportunity where they find it to foster Radical Connection. One way to do so is by bringing their values to the forefront: by embracing the triple bottom line. Through aligning with their customers and the community in meaningful ways extending far beyond dollars and cents, they hope to create the deep, visceral bond indicative of Radical Connection.

In Chapter 5 we included a chart listing the attributes differentiating transactional and Radical Connection. Several have direct application to companies seeking to embrace the triple bottom line. One especially stands out.

DEEP CONNECTION

By its nature, a transactional relationship remains on the *surface*, a considerable problem for a stockbroker such as TD Ameritrade; their business is transactional as they process clients' trades. When the connection remains superficial, a business risks losing its customer to a rival based on factors such as pricing. After all, if the only real connection is based on little more than transactions and a competitor has similar features and cheaper prices, *why not move*? This is especially problematic in the present era of internet-based brokerages, which often entice investors with appealing offers.

Going beyond surface-level interactions therefore offers a strategic advantage for companies in many industries. As we know by now, Radical Connection enables deep affiliation toward an organization—an emotional or visceral bond. For-profit companies wishing to tap into these powerful feelings achieve Radical Connection when they show they care about the same goals and values as their customers and other stakeholders. In the case of TD Ameritrade, financially literate investors who gained their knowledge from the efforts of the brokerage are bound to feel a deep affinity to it. They are also more inclined to work with a company they might not otherwise, especially if not for the efforts of the Changing Your World consulting team.

A win-win for the triple bottom line, for sure.

INDUCING JOY, MEANING, AND PURPOSE

Again, transactional connections remain neutral for most stakeholders. We don't feel strongly positive about many products and services we so often use; instead, we just need them to get through our days. For example, do you feel a sense of joy and meaning when you choose one gas station over another? Or are you simply focused on the price at the pump as well as how easy it will be to get back on the right road? Once upon a time, so-called legacy businesses hoped to foster a stronger connection by performing tasks particularly well. In the case of TD Ameritrade, this meant providing strong customer service and industry-leading tools to investors. But these advantages only go so far in creating relationships with additional stakeholders, especially when the competition starts to catch up.

Radical Connection, however, produces overwhelmingly positive feelings to customers and other stakeholders. People experience joy and a sense of meaning and purpose, for example, when they know their hard-earned money is contributing to educating others about financial literacy. This is especially true when they consider how the recipients of such knowledge might otherwise be trapped in a death spiral of consumer debt. No doubt, it's the same sense of purpose Bombas shoppers feel when they know buying a pair of comfortable socks will result in a pair reaching the hands of a homeless person. Importantly, this feeling isn't constrained only to customers. As we shared in Chapter 3, employees radically connected to a company feel happier going to work and are more likely to rebuff efforts to poach them away.

HOW SOMETHING CAN BECOME PART OF YOUR LEGACY

Transactional connections happen fast and are then forgotten. Think again about the example of stopping to fill up your gas tank. In a week, will you remember which station you stopped at? Probably not. Most people will forget such a transaction the very same day. In the case of investing, customers with a transactional relationship will often have to sort through multiple accounts with different brokerages to find a particular holding or trade just because their connection is so superficial, they don't differentiate between various faceless businesses in their mind.

Radical Connection provides the exact opposite experience. If the transactional connection is the gas station we forget about, Radical Connection is the destination we can't wait to reach. In the case of this attribute, it's about the organization we are radically connected to becoming a part of our legacy. Naturally, wealth accumulated through investing is a legacy in itself, but few people define themselves entirely by their net worth. Instead, TD Ameritrade is now engaged in showing customers, employees, and other stakeholders that they really are co-participating in improving the financial literacy of underserved communities.

And bettering lives. The ability to say "I contributed to more people understanding money" is a legacy builder to many investors, and a powerful corporate incentive today's nonprofits can learn from.

EVEN SO, SOCIAL RESPONSIBILITY MUST BE DONE RIGHT

By now we know companies embracing CSR as more than a marketing ploy must take their responsibilities to the triple bottom line to heart. Highlighting the rapid growth of CSR, a report by the Governance & Accountability Institute found that 86% of S&P 500 Index companies published sustainability or CSR reports in 2018, compared with fewer than 20% in 2011. For many, ethical and mission-driven capitalism pays dividends in critical ways. Then again, when organizations aren't sincere, instead viewing social responsibility as a cynical marketing play, disaster lurks around the corner.

The world's largest shoe brand learned this the hard way. Nike has been a progressive company for years. During all this time, it claimed to care about the workers in its supply chain. Yet so much professing blew up in the outfitter's face at the close of the 20th century when customers who once felt Radical Connection to the "mission-driven company" learned the sad truth: Nike was using sweatshop labor to produce its beloved shoes.

The Guardian published a story titled, "Nike Accused of Tolerating Sweatshops" on May 19, 2001, outlining the claims against the company:

A new report, Still Waiting For Nike To Do It, published by the San Francisco-based Global Exchange, says Nike workers still toil for excessive hours in high-pressure work environments while not earning enough to meet the basic needs of their children.

The report's findings will further embarrass a company already discredited by consumer groups for exploitation of labour.

In 1996 Nike was severely embarrassed when a US magazine featured a photograph of a young Pakistani boy sewing together a Nike football. The following year it was revealed that workers in one of its contracted factories in Vietnam were being exposed to toxic fumes at up to 177 times the Vietnamese legal limit.

Clearly, making claims of social responsibility that are not part of a company's DNA *and* expressed in every business decision is a poor way to avoid controversy. However, being truly mission-driven and "walking the walk" when it comes to social responsibility is more effective than ever. Evidence from the recent COVID-19 pandemic illustrates this extremely well.

Institutional Investor reported on the performance of philanthrocapitalism in an April 2021 article titled "Here's More Evidence That ESG Funds Outperformed During the Pandemic." Author Will Feuer explains: "In the first year of the pandemic, large funds with environmental, social, and governance criteria outperformed the broader market, according to a report published this week by S&P Global. It's the latest of such analyses to suggest that ESG risks matter for investment performance, at least during a pandemic. S&P's analysis included 26 ESG exchange-traded funds and mutual funds with more than $250 million in assets under management. From March 5, 2020, to March 5, 2021, 19 of the funds grew between 27.3 percent and 55 percent, outpacing the S&P 500 index's 27.1 percent rise, according to S&P."

Although brands must be sincere in their approach to mission and ethics, it's increasingly impossible for them to ignore the subject altogether. Consumer survey data gathered by Porter Novelli, a global communications firm, says that "62% believe a company's purpose is an important factor when making a quick or impulse purchase. 71% would purchase from a purpose-driven company over the alternative when cost and quality are equal. 78% are more likely to remember a company with a strong purpose." (This is according to Porter Novelli's 2021 Purpose Perception Study, an online survey to assess something seemingly qualitative, that gut feeling we have when we emotionally align with a mission.) Research from Harvard Business School professor Elizabeth Keenan bears this out. Keenan wrote that "consumers are a lot more informed about what firms are doing, so it's important to be authentic in your giving because consumers seek out the information and will start making comparisons on their own."

HOW TO KEEP THINGS AUTHENTIC

The best way to ensure authenticity is to align a company's mission with its core business and competencies. TD Ameritrade is not providing food to the hungry or planting trees because those activities aren't related to the company's primary operations. Instead, they are teaching people financial literacy, a mission directly aligned with the company's main business processes. Likewise, Panera Bread is feeding people instead of teaching them about investing or providing clothes for the homeless. This alignment creates a natural synergy between sustainability and the core business.

Another example of this alignment is CVS, one of America's largest drug store chains. CEO Karen Lynch has been referred to by *Fortune* as "the most powerful woman in American business."

She earned this vaunted reputation in part by being an outspoken advocate of improving America's broken health care system and putting her company and its resources toward the mission of improving care for *all* Americans, regardless of wealth level.

Although the CVS plan is multifaceted, we'd like to draw attention to two portions. First, Lynch points out there are more CVS locations than hospitals in this country. Moving forward, she plans for many or most stores to mimic the services of walk-in clinics, creating a system of frontline care locations within 10 miles of every person in the country. Second, CVS is jumping into the telehealth space with a "digital-first, technology-forward approach" designed to provide better remote care and lower costs.

These initiatives and more are designed to improve the health equity of the country, directly benefiting the triple bottom line. More important, the steps are extensions of what CVS is already good at—dealing with Americans of all walks of life who have health concerns. Lynch has reimagined her company from a typical retail empire into one dedicated to both making money *and* helping individuals, including those who might not even be customers. The authenticity of the CVS mission is inevitable because it is so closely aligned with its business operations.

WHY NONPROFITS SHOULD EMBRACE SOCIALLY RESPONSIBLE COMPANIES

Many nonprofits are beginning to realize the value of their mission-driven counterparts. Still, some may view them as competition attempting to edge them out of the market, in other words, like a traditional rival in the for-profit economy. This is the wrong way to look at these companies. Their missions typically entail vast problems with a pervasive impact on humanity. It would be virtually impossible for a corporation to wholly own such a grand purpose. The focus instead should be on finding ways to collaborate for the benefit of all.

Nonprofits can (and should) pursue radical partnerships with socially responsible companies. In fact, opportunities are essentially limitless as more corporations adopt the triple bottom line. These partnerships are often unexpected and require outside-the-box thinking to put together. For example, The Lego Group has stated its desire to go carbon-neutral in the future. This may seem crazy for a company generating large amounts of plastic, but a nonprofit focused on reforestation could indeed partner with Lego to create a huge win-win relationship. This is an emergent phenomenon, that is, when the right corporation partners with the right nonprofit, the math becomes $1 + 1 = 3$.

Truly, the sky is the limit when it comes to these partnerships. Consider some groups discussed in this chapter. TD Ameritrade teamed up with 4-H on its financial literacy program, but other nonprofits could also collaborate with the stockbroker to service more communities. Also, 4-H is largely unknown within urban environments. Couldn't a nonprofit focused on young people in a major metro area create a similar partnership, piggybacking on the experience and learnings from the original project? In the case of CVS, which aims to create a network of clinics within its stores, couldn't nonprofits devoted to providing free clinics help the company achieve its goal of improving health equity by a partnership in population-dense areas? With egos aside and a commitment to systemic change, there's a seemingly endless number of synergies in which nonprofits and corporations could work together to accelerate their purpose-driven work to create a better world.

BUT NEVER FORGET THE EMPLOYEES

Purpose-driven companies with strong CSRs and an emphasis on the triple bottom line also benefit from having more engaged staff and a stronger recruiting and retention proposition. It makes sense if you think about it—consumers are demanding values and a positive mission from the companies they buy products and services from. Why wouldn't they expect the very same from the companies they work for?

Having a strong sense of values and mission is in fact one of the key solutions to the Great Resignation. By now it's common knowledge that millions of people quit their jobs in the post-pandemic economy. But the Great Resignation was due purely to the dollars and cents of compensation; it's also a reflection—and reckoning—of toxic workplaces, bad bosses, and companies that only care about one bottom line: profits. Yet, when a company has a strong sense of mission and purpose like TD Ameritrade, employees become more connected. There is no need to join the Great Resignation when you work for leaders who understand how to balance successful business practices while also doing good.

Additionally, companies with strong purpose tend to attract employees with the same sense of mission. These workers are good investments—they are strong performers and are not likely to be recruited away when they believe in the company's raison d'etre. At the same time, people who are more engaged in their work generally lead more productive existences in all facets of life. If you admire the engaged workforces of companies such as Patagonia, Panera, and TD Ameritrade, please understand they don't have a secret sauce when it comes to recruiting; they just have strong missions, a purpose-driven approach to business, and strong corporate cultures valuing employees. People want to be associated with brands that do good in the world. This applies to whom people buy from—and whom they work for. In both cases, this truth translates into better outcomes for society. In Chapter 8 we'll turn our focus toward the personal benefits of solving our Generosity Crisis.

Making Generosity Personal

There is a tendency for us to take a cynical view toward giving. Would Mark Zuckerberg *really* devote so much of his fortune to philanthropy if he couldn't do so in the form of the CZI, the LLC he formed to preserve his corporate power while gaining immense tax benefits? Would Bill Gates *really* put so much of his time and wealth toward charity if he didn't gain immense notoriety based on the works of The Bill & Melinda Gates Foundation? We can endlessly debate these cases and many similar examples, but the fact is, we know the answer to this question in at least one case.

We needn't look further than the man dubbed the James Bond of Philanthropy by *The New York Times*. Just the mention of James Bond may have you humming the iconic theme song from the long-running movie series. If so, good! The tale of Chuck Feeney, our 007 of philanthropy, is best enjoyed with his namesake's theme playing. Feeney struck it rich in 1960 when he founded the DutyFree Shoppers Group (DFS Group) with several partners. He pulled in massive earnings selling luxury goods to travelers with a particular emphasis on the Asian market. According to *The Wall Street Journal*, DFS Group was generating more than $300 million in profits a year by the 1990s.

But Feeney was keeping a secret from his partners—he was no longer the owner of his nearly 40% stake in the company. Apparently, in the early 1980s, Feeney transferred his stake in DFS Group and the vast bulk of his personal wealth to a charitable foundation he created called The Atlantic Philanthropies. Since then, the foundation had been covertly donating his wealth to charities all over the globe, ranging from Cornell University to public health programs in Vietnam.

His giving was so clandestine, though, that The Atlantic Philanthropies usually stipulated recipients did not disclose the donation source.

Over the years, Feeney has given away an astounding $8 billion, much of which occurred before his charitable activities ever came to light. When it did reach public consciousness and Feeney was asked why he gave away so much of his money—in secret, no less—he stated, "I believe strongly in giving while living. I see little reason to delay giving when so much good can be achieved through supporting worthwhile causes today. Besides, it's a lot more fun to give while you live than to give while you are dead."

As it turns out, Feeney gave away *billions* of dollars under the cloak of darkness. But he didn't dispense his largesse to get on TV or even to be heralded some magnanimous thought leader. He also didn't do it for cheeky tax purposes or for some yet unrealized financial benefit. He did it out of his Radical Connection to organizations, nonprofits, and communities that so enriched his family. Feeney's own explanation of his life's work is captured in a letter he wrote to Bill Gates in 2011. His thoughts are instructive on how Radical Connection and the generosity that follows it can benefit your own life.

Feeney wrote, "The process of—and most importantly, the results from—granting this wealth to good causes has been a rich source of joy and satisfaction to me and for my family. . . .The challenges, even setbacks, I have experienced in my decades of personal engagement in philanthropy pale in comparison to the impact and deep personal satisfaction."

PERSONALLY GAINING BY EMBRACING RADICAL CONNECTION

Feeney enjoyed the "deep personal satisfaction" of his generosity. He surely got a kick out of doing it in the shadows, too—but the point is, he realized by 1982 that giving without strings was a central part of his life, and he helped to change the world for the positive. The authors of this book each enjoyed brushes with Radical Connection at an early age, shifting the trajectory of their own lives and setting them on course to give back in meaningful ways.

Giving the Actual Shirt Off Your Back

Coauthor Brian grew up in a culture of service and philanthropy. Through high school and later at St. John's University, volunteering at soup kitchens in Brooklyn, shelving deliveries to the local food pantry, and raising money for worthy causes were just another part of normal life for Brian and his friends and family. His devotion to service made him a natural fit to apply to join the President's Society as a college ambassador.

The President's Society ambassador is one of the most prestigious student roles at St. John's University. It's also difficult to achieve. As college ambassadors, the President's Society travels with the university president to show the world what type of students St. John's produces. After several rounds of interviews, Brian learned he was a finalist for this most coveted of positions. It all came down to one more critical interview before the university's board of trustees.

Thrilled by this opportunity, Brian wore his best suit on the big day. He was nervous, but prepared—and remembers the interview like it was yesterday. Of the many questions the trustees threw at Brian, one stands out above the rest: "What does St. John's University mean to you?"

Brian replied without a pause: "St. John's means always doing the right thing. It usually isn't easy and sometimes takes time to figure out the best way to handle a problem but doing the right thing for people and God is what I view as the St. John's way. Every day I take pride in 'walking the walk' instead of just 'talking the talk.'"

What Brian didn't know was that he would be given just the chance to walk the walk once he left the conference room. But first, you should know Brian felt good exiting his interview. He hadn't pinned his whole identity on being accepted to the President's Society. He was just glad he made it this far. In fact, he felt like it was a huge win to have made it to the finals. Exiting with a bounce to his step, Brian noticed an unusual scene unfolding at administrative secretary Mrs. Smith's desk. Fellow classmate Larry Sartori, also a finalist for the President's Society, stood beside her looking sweaty and flustered coming in late from his work responsibilities. (Note: we fictionalized the names in this story.)

Brian could hear the distress in Larry's voice as he drew nearer. "But Mrs. Smith, my boss needed me to finish up a time-sensitive project and I ran over here as quickly as I could. I can't go in front of the board of trustees in . . . *my sweaty work clothes and without my suit on!*"

Mrs. Smith, who had heard just about every flimsy excuse a student could dream up, looked unphased by Larry's plea. "Mr. Sartori, you are either in front of the board for your finalist interview in 10 minutes, or you can forget about the President's Society."

Brian stopped dead in his tracks.

Dressed in the best suit he had ever owned, he looked at Larry in his sweaty outfit and sneakers. *Is it fair Larry's obligations to his team should interfere with his chance to make the President's Society?* The irony also wasn't lost on Brian. He had just told the trustees that St. John's is about "walking the walk." Now he was being tested by his own words. Smiling at his classmate, Brian said, "Hey Larry, we're close enough to the same size. Follow me to the bathroom. You can borrow my suit for your interview. Splash some water on your face and you'll be good as new."

Larry couldn't believe his luck. (Neither could Mrs. Smith.)

"Wow, Brian, you're really saving my life here," he said.

Then the boys quickly put Brian's plan into action, swapping clothes in the precious minutes before Larry's interview. Afterward, Brian sat in the lobby, waiting patiently while wearing Larry's sweaty clothes and enduring curious looks from all those passing through. Meanwhile, Larry wowed the trustees in Brian's suit, which enabled both of them to be chosen as part of this highly selective group of college ambassadors. And Brian came away from the experience with a deep sense of pride and an experience that is part of the Radical Connection he has for his alma mater.

Reflecting on the incident all these year later, Brian feels positive about what happened that day. "I was radically connected to St. John's—and still am. I believed in its mission, and I knew I couldn't deprive a fellow student of the chance to become a college ambassador just because of the circumstances he found himself in. I hope and believe I acted in good faith to my own values and those of the university."

Joining a Sandwich Assembly Line

By no means was coauthor Nathan born with a silver spoon in his mouth. Yet even in a lower-income single-parent household, Nathan always had reliable access to food. To Nathan and his friends, many of whom were in the same income bracket, hunger was understood as little more than the unpleasant feeling right before dinner time. Looking back at those days, Nathan tells us, "Even though we didn't have much, we never missed a meal out of need. Somehow, we always got by, but as a child I had the awareness, and sometimes fear, that with a bad string of luck, that our circumstances could change. Growing up with a deep appreciation for the basic elements of life, in high school I had an opportunity to serve the homeless in downtown Los Angeles and it really opened my eyes."

What Nathan observed as a high school freshman was the daily experience of people lacking the privilege of food security. On Skid Row Nathan saw homeless people as well as a mobile soup kitchen serving not only adults but also teens and small children.

In that moment he realized how something he took for granted—food available at predictable mealtimes—wasn't so easy for people just an hour away from his home.

The experience had such an impact on the teen that he acted immediately to do his part for the community. More importantly, he began searching for a way to directly contribute to the hunger problem in Los Angeles. By sophomore year he found it. By sheer happenstance, Nathan found after-school employment for a small legal services firm in his community. Serendipitously, the owner and his wife had just established a robust plan to address food insecurity in one of LA's neediest areas.

Nathan enthusiastically joined their ranks, devoting his Saturdays to the cause. He and his friends would drive down to a house owned by a family member near Lafayette Park in downtown LA in the morning, then spend hours preparing and wrapping sandwiches. The ingredients varied week to week because the teens would collect donations from stores in the suburbs, making up for whatever was missing by using their own money and small donations.

It wasn't long before Nathan and his friends became expert sandwich makers. Instead of working hourly jobs, they became an all-volunteer assembly line devoted to producing portable meals for the needy. After completing their sandwiches, the group would split into teams wheeling around a shopping cart full of their creations, distributing food to whoever needed it. Despite his passion, this wasn't at all easy for Nathan. It was the first time he had ever spoken to homeless people and he felt nervous to break the ice.

Yet in no time at all, what little shyness Nathan had melted away. He began conversing with those he was feeding. He found they needed to know someone cared enough to speak to them just as much as they needed the sandwich he prepared. Nathan explains, "I now know that I was Radically Connected to that group feeding people in downtown LA. I remember going on vacation one time, which caused me to miss a Saturday. . . it was like a pain in my chest. I've been passionate about helping others for my entire life based on those first years with our ragtag sandwich army."

Becoming a Santa Claus in Training

Coauthor Michael grew up halfway across the country from Nathan. His family lived a comfortable life in a nice suburb of St. Louis, Missouri. By no means rich, his family was also never so short on money that food was a problem. Likewise, Michael recalls that he usually got the gifts he asked for at Christmas and on his birthday. When Michael was 12 years old, his family changed the way it celebrated Christmas, and the experience created a strong sense of service and charity in Michael existing to this day.

Sometime before Christmas, Michael's mom explained to his little brother and him that they would perform the normal Christmas Day activities differently that year. Rather than just open their own presents and play with them all day like usual, the three would venture into the city to help a needy family. At the time this happened, Michael's parents were divorced. According to the custody arrangement, his mom got to be with him and his brother during this holiday time of year. Through some friends, Michael's mom had joined a program pairing families like his with underprivileged ones in the downtown area. His family would "adopt" another that attended a participating church.

After opening their own gifts at home, Michael's mom drove him and his brother to the church so they could spend Christmas Day with this other family, providing them with some of the joy of their own Christmas experience. Michael remembers being cautious about the plan when he first heard it. "To be honest, my first concern was spending the special holiday with strangers—what if they were weird or mean? But the decision was already made, and at 12 years old, I knew to get on board."

Christmas morning went off without a hitch in Michael's household. He and his little brother loved their presents, especially the Vanilla Ice cassette tape they got that year. After their normal celebration concluded early, the two boys learned there was a bit more work to do. They needed to wrap presents for the family they would spend Christmas with: a mother and her two kids, one boy and one girl around Michael's age. His mom had bought some of the gifts and others were donated by parishioners, but all needed wrapping. Eventually, after opening and playing with their new toys, they headed downtown.

That day, Michael's mom drove him and his brother deep into the city, a poor area they had never seen before. Here they met the family they were paired with. Despite whatever misgivings Michael and his brother might have had going into this meeting, they quickly vanished. The kids were very nice and eager to play with them. They loved their presents and were grateful to be included in Michael's family tradition of eating at a Chinese restaurant. This was the first time they had ever eaten Asian food and loved it. The restaurant was a big hit, and everyone became more comfortable over crab rangoon and eggrolls. It was time to share some gifts, and Michael and his brother Kevin felt a sudden urge to take over proceedings, what they called being a "Santa Claus in training."

Michael grabbed the pile of gifts and distributed one to the mom. Then his brother followed, handing out toys for the boy and girl. As the family opened their gifts one by one, Michael noticed the happiness on their faces. Though the presents were relatively modest, they unleashed such joy. A powerful feeling built within Michael and Kevin. Reflecting on the event years later, Michael explains, "I realized I was really blessed to have what I considered to be an ordinary life. I also learned to be happy with what I had, because others could be content with much less." Like his coauthors, this event left a big mark on Michael's life. Not only did his family continue the tradition but also he has made plans for a similar event as his own children get a little older. He explains, "I want to instill the same feelings of generosity and gratitude in my kids that my mom instilled in me."

HELPING OURSELVES—THROUGH HELPING OTHERS

Each author's story shows how their lives improved by helping others. Although none are (so far!) billionaires affecting drastic changes on a societal level, each can look back on seminal experiences had when they were young. These moments and the positive feelings they evoked improved the lives of others. They also improved their own lives. When we give back, we are beneficiaries to our own gratitude. We gain happiness, purpose, and a sense of mission. In fact, the positivity gained from philanthropy is so powerful that it can have a lasting impact on deeply negative states of being such as depression.

Dr. Seth Gillihan explains in a *Psychology Today* article that researchers recently examined how generosity affects depression with a study that created specific goals for participants to focus on, broadly grouped as "self-image goals" and "compassionate goals." The self-image variety included activities such as "avoiding showing any weakness," and compassionate goals included deeds such as "making a positive difference in someone else's life."

When the results of focusing on these different goals were compared, the answer was clear. The researchers found that dwelling on self-image goals worsened depression symptoms during the six-week study. Worse, they also caused relationship conflicts. Yet when compassionate goals remained paramount, depression symptoms lessened, and the participants also experienced fewer relationship conflicts.

Gillihan summarized the findings in his article: "The really good news is that by turning our attention toward helping others, we make everyone feel better—ourselves included. We find not only relief from our depression and anxiety, but also improvements in our relationships. Taken together, these two effects can trigger a 'virtuous circle' in which improved relationships lead to feeling better, which leads to improved relationships, and so forth."

The best news of all? The virtuous circle Gillihan describes is not just limited to those fighting depression and anxiety. Generosity is fantastic game changer in a multitude of ways. Let's investigate them now.

IT LEADS TO PERSONAL HEALTH BENEFITS

Greater Good Magazine explains generosity is good for our personal health. Study after study, including one completed in 2008 by Harvard Business School professor Michael Norton, demonstrates that giving money to another person—instead of spending it on ourselves—improves happiness, but only if we have a choice in the matter. Happiness expert and professor Sonja Lyubomirsky achieved a similar result in a study in which participants were asked to complete multiple acts of kindness each week in a six-week program. Turns out that these joyful feelings—the "warm glow" felt by each author when they acted altruistically in their youth—don't just represent a random or nebulous phenomenon. Rather, they are intimately tied to our neurochemistry.

Researchers at the National Institutes of Health found in a 2006 study that giving to charities activates the brain's pleasure region. Acting philanthropically also activates the sections associated with social connection and trust. Should you reflect on the author stories in this chapter, you'll find they each experienced a similar reaction to acting generously. *Psychology Today* has an explanation for this. Doing good causes the brain to release endorphins just as it does with physical exercise, producing positive feelings throughout the body. The resulting euphoria after one's generous actions is often referred to as the "helper's high."

To this point, *Time* documents in a 2017 article titled "Being Generous Really Does Make You Happier" how generosity leads to greater happiness, which in turn improves clinical outcomes and promotes longer lifespans. Philippe Tobler, professor at the University of Zurich and lead author of a generosity study, explains in the same piece that older people who are giving tend to enjoy better health, adding, "Moreover, there is a positive association between helping others and life expectancy, perhaps because helping others reduces stress." Tobler's research demonstrates that even *pledging* to take generous actions has beneficial outcomes, explaining that "making a commitment to help others is a first step to follow through."

It Builds and Strengthens Communities

Generosity is a basic building block essential to societal functioning. Although giving isn't limited to religious communities, their various structures provide effective examples of how generosity has improved people's lives for millennia. One such example is tzedakah, the Jewish tradition of making charity endemic to daily life. The *Jewish Virtual Library* explains how deeply the act of tzedakah is engrained into the functioning of traditional Jewish communities:

> Life in the shtetl [the small villages of Eastern Europe] begins and ends with tzedakah. When a child is born,

the father pledges a certain amount of money for distribution to the poor. At a funeral the mourners distrib-
ute coins to the beggars who swarm the cemetery,
chanting, "Tzedakah saves from death."

At every turn during one's life, the reminder to give
is present. . . If something good or bad happens, one
puts a coin into a box. Before lighting the Sabbath can-
dles, the housewife drops a coin into one of the boxes. . .
Children are trained to the habit of giving. A father will
have his son give alms to the beggar instead of handing
them over directly. A child is very often put in charge of
the weekly dole at home when beggars make their cus-
tomary rounds. The gesture of giving becomes almost
a reflex. (Mark Zborowski and Elizabeth Herzog, *Life
Is with People*)

Of course, the Christian faith has its own strong tradition of
giving. Tithing (giving 10% of one's income to the church) is one
such example. This custom is so strong that none other than
national financial radio host and bestselling author Dave Ramsey
discusses tithing with every caller who identifies as a Christian.
Although Ramsey's stance on personal finances is built on
destroying debt, he doesn't advise Christians to stop tithing even
when facing a mountain of their own. In his mind, tithing
strengthens the church, which also builds relational bonds, benefiting the group and the individual who chooses to give.

As Ramsey explained to someone who wrote to him for
advice, published in the *Chester County Independent* on this subject, "Tithing isn't about making a deposit into God's bank
account or building up spiritual brownie points. It isn't a salva-
tion issue, either. It's all about changing our hearts and our
minds. It's about being a little less selfish, and a little more

Christ-like. I believe it makes God smile when we put other people's needs ahead of our own wants."

Of course, generosity's role in strengthening community extends beyond religious institutions. Consider the example of a cancer walk in a community park. The well-attended event draws people in who might not know each other initially. Yet by participating and coming together, they can create new strong bonds of interdependence due to their mutual resolve to fight this disease.

Events of all sizes have the potential to strengthen interpersonal bonds. In 2001, coauthor Nathan joined his local Rotary Club chapter, which holds an annual Lobster Fest bringing in more than 1,000 hungry people from his community and also nearby towns. As Nathan explains, "They come for the all-you-can-eat lobster, but they stay for the community, making new friends and memories." As president of the chapter several years ago, Nathan learned the event also brings in hundreds of thousands of dollars, all of which goes toward worthy local causes. This is another form of a virtuous cycle that generosity produces for the collective good.

Incidentally, philanthropy needn't be as formal as a cancer walk or a Rotary Club event to strengthen community bonds. The trend of paying it forward has led to the emergent phenomenon of spontaneous acts of small-scale generosity. A common example? Learning in the coffee shop drive-thru line that the car ahead of you paid for your morning latte. This simple act has the power to turn a mundane morning into an oasis of happiness— and it's happening a million times a day across the country in various ways. Random acts of kindness improve community bonds, even if the community in question is as specific as the patrons of a particular coffee shop.

Crowdfunding

Crowdfunding once began as a way for entrepreneurs to launch new products and services by raising the capital through an internet appeal for support. Think Kickstarter. It wasn't long before generosity affected its own positive spin as more people turned to the web not just to launch their cat-themed calendar or newest tech gizmo but also to get financial help in desperate times such as illness or death. A funny thing happened along the way— complete strangers began contributing to help others through their toughest times.

Moreover, the market for social crowdfunding has exploded. According to *Statista*, $17.2 billion in crowdfunding occurred just within North America in 2021. That's a 33.7% increase from the year before, and all signs point to crowdfunding growing in the coming years. Though digital in nature, crowdfunding strengthens existing communities, bringing together strangers. A 2017 article in *Forbes* examines the crowdfunding campaign begun in support of Laura Napolitano, a medical researcher and physician struck by early-onset Alzheimer's. Her crowdfunding campaign exemplifies our points. It raised $21,000 of its $25,000 goal in a year, helping to ensure Napolitano would receive adequate care. Donors, including those who had never met Napolitano, now receive regular updates on her condition via the YouCaring crowdfunding platform.

To be sure, analog versions of crowdfunding existed long before the internet enabled its current iteration. Nathan witnessed it firsthand in his low-income, single-parent home. His family's house developed a roof leak that they could not afford to fix. After learning of their troubles, a concerned group of 10 men from their church came over to fix it for free, bringing all the necessary supplies to pull off the feat. Their kind actions made an impression on 7-year-old Nathan, who learned to use a hammer while watching, vowing to give back by contributing his time and efforts to Habitat for Humanity.

Zoos/Theatres/Arts/Films/Performances

In the first part of this book, we explored how culture plays a major role in every community. We all possess fuller, richer lives because of key institutions such as zoos, theatres, art museums, and other related organizations. As customers, we may support these nonprofits with our ticket purchases, but such sales only go so far. When you instead become a monthly patron at a zoo or theatre, you're helping to pay it forward, enabling these resources to touch the hearts and minds of future generations. When we have positive childhood memories of the zoo or the theatre, we strengthen our community by ensuring more children will experience such fond, constructive memories.

These positive cultural institutions carry on their good works in large part because benefactors support them. As discussed, the public's tendency is to blindly assume a small group of wealthy individuals will support these nonprofits with multimillion-dollar donations. But it just isn't that simple, especially during our Generosity Crisis. This is not something for other, wealthier people to take on solely—*each* person would do well to play their part in ensuring our cultural institutions and landmarks exist in perpetuity.

Here's one example. Brian donates every year to the Torch Fund, the annual giving program of Chaminade High School. Donations to this organization are used to build the high school's development fund, which generates earnings to defray tuition costs for boys attending the high school. In 2022, contributions to the Torch Fund help offset $2,340 in tuition for each student.

Brian so values the education he received at Chaminade that he wants to ensure the private school's tuition does not stand in the way of producing a steady stream of Chaminade men now—and well into the future.

LET'S NOT LEAVE OUT THE BENEFITS TO FAMILY BONDS

Just as society has become more atomized, families cannot escape the same problem of breakdown. Parents with teens have become used to the phenomenon of four people sitting in a room, each staring at their screens with only the family dog paying attention to everyone. Could giving combat this feeling of separation by strengthening altruistic family traditions? Yes. Teaching kids the benefits of helping others brings family units closer together, especially reminding little ones of the value of gratitude, to appreciate what they have.

As *Fidelity Charitable* explains, "Philanthropy can be a powerful way for families to pass along their shared beliefs and values. It can also provide unique opportunities for families to spend time together, collaborate, and learn more about one another. Integrating philanthropic conversations and activities into family life is an excellent way to encourage healthy attitudes about helping others while instilling a sense of financial responsibility among younger generations. And giving together can be a bonding experience for family members of all generations."

A wide range of activities are available that can integrate generosity into a family's traditions. For example, philanthropic acts can be in honor of a family member who has passed away. Also, a family can discuss what organizations to donate time and money to, giving everyone a say. This creates a sense of mission and investment for the whole clan, as well as strengthening bonds and values. Some families can even make a charitable grant to a child's favorite charity a reward for good grades and other positive behaviours.

It Aids the Environment (People *and* Nature)

Some of us make the mistake of taking a 30,000-foot view of environmental issues. When you concentrate on carbon emissions and other pollutants, regular people seem helpless to fix the issue. After all, what can one person do to change the state's energy grid? Yet if we zoom in to the local level, we can see there are ways to improve the environment, both for nature *and* for people. For example, local solutions addressing homelessness provide others with adequate shelter, reduce illness due to exposure to the elements, and return public spaces once cluttered with tents and temporary shelter to the public. Such actions strengthen the community while treating all people with the respect they deserve.

Quite often, acts of generosity improve both nature and humanity in a non-exclusive manner. For example, when non-profits organize trash cleanups in public places, they enhance conditions for local wildlife while also enhancing the community's enjoyment of nature. When people travel to a public park, they hope to enjoy the serenity of unspoiled greenery, not have to tiptoe through broken glass and other litter. A rising tide lifts all ships so that communities improve when we collectively clean the litter up, instead of just chiding the litterer. Just as being a good citizen can strengthen community bonds, being a caring one can also fortify the connections between humanity and the environment.

YOUR GENEROSITY HOMEWORK?

You may not have expected homework when you started reading this book, but you're getting some anyway. Your assignment is simple—look in the mirror. Generosity starts with you. As authors, we know that the tendency as a reader is to study the ideas in a book, learning how they apply to others. But this material is also about *you*. It's a safe bet you want a better world, both for today and for future generations. This world is made possible through generosity, but it isn't *guaranteed*. Although philanthropy is changing, getting involved, pitching in, and helping is within *everyone's* power. And as we have said all along, giving is not as much a function of wealth (how much you give) but rather a willingness to help, for the love for humankind.

In the next chapter, we'll explore how tech can also be a force for greater philanthropy and kindness, not just another driver of our Generosity Crisis.

CHAPTER 9

Creating Radical Connection with Emerging Tech

Irving Kaplan met the love of his life while puking his guts out. The year was 1952. For weeks, his friend Marty had begged him to come to a community dance to be put on by City of Hope in Los Angeles.

"It'll be great," said Marty. "Good food. Great music. *Pretty women.*"

Irving liked the sound of that. He was 22 and single, and he envisioned the lively soirée as a chance to show off dance moves he learned back in cotillion. The day before, he spent his paycheck on a new suit and tie, convinced he would turn heads on the big night. As for the charity itself? Irving had heard something about how the funds raised from the evening went to help sick people suffering from tuberculosis. That was good, too.

Only things didn't pan out like Irving expected. The afternoon of the big night he started feeling queasy. He attributed it to nerves, passing on the porkchops served to the 300 assembled in the hotel ballroom.

"Aren't you gonna eat?" Marty asked between bites.

"Nah."

Instead, Irving scanned the room, making mental notes of which lovely lady to approach just as soon as they cleared the tables. But then his body betrayed him. He felt bile in the back of his throat. Seconds later, he rushed out, heading for the bathroom. He didn't make it. Irving threw up the contents of his stomach on the plush hallway carpet. *Must be food poisoning*, he thought to himself.

He felt the hand on his neck before he ever heard her sweet voice.

"You okay?"

Embarrassed, he wiped his mouth and looked up.

"Barbara looked like an angel. The most beautiful creature I ever saw," Irving told people for the rest of his life.

Within weeks, Irving and Barbara wed. Not only did they never forget City of Hope as the reason they met, it became the center of their social life. They joined the charity, organizing future fundraisers at their synagogue. They also attended the gala the next year, celebrating it as a second anniversary—made all the sweeter for Irving since he could enjoy the meal this time.

The Kaplans instilled their love of City of Hope into their kids in the ensuing years. Some of their daughter Kim's happiest early memories were the charity tea parties Barbara hosted. When his son Ned came of age, Irving advised him to also find someone at the same gala where his parents met. His encouragement paid off. Ned met his wife while working the auction booth.

Part of their history, City of Hope gave them identities. Kim and Ned encouraged their kids to give to the organization and volunteer, establishing memories at events like the gala year after year. It became their community and tradition, too, defining their family: Who they were and what they valued.

Transforming Tech: From a Problem to a Solution

The story of how Irving and Barbara met, and the subsequent role City of Hope played in the Kaplan family, may seem strange to today's youth. In a world of dating apps and social media, attending a dance hoping to meet an eligible single person seems impossibly quaint. (Try it with a young person yourself—they're likely to think you are playing an elaborate joke with them as the punchline.) This is how much tech has changed our society.

But it isn't all bad news. Innovation can also help us restore generosity to its rightful place. It can bring people together IRL (in real life) leading to unprecedented Radical Connection. Seriously. Let us explain. Technology is a tool. Like any tool, it's not inherently good or bad. Unfortunately, the negative applications of recent technology, such as social media's addictiveness, have proven to be very profitable, leading so-called surveillance capitalists to exploit users as the products themselves (especially via the attention economy).

Now for the flip side. Savvy nonprofits can harness existing innovations and those emerging soon as forces for good. In fact, they *must* harness technologies to meet consumer expectations and continue their good work far into the future. Fortunately, some cutting-edge exemplars have been utilizing tech to answer two of the central problems of the Generosity Crisis since well before 2020. We call these problems the *relationship quandary* and the *reaching young people quandary*.

The Relationship Quandary

As discussed, nonprofits relying on in-person events to win and keep relationships struggled mightily when galas and the like evaporated in the wake of COVID-19. The problem was compounded by how many nonprofits had taken their donors for granted. For years. Focused on revenue as their primary goal, too many charities assumed donations would flow whether or not they invested in nurturing authentic relationships with donors.

Instead, the result of de-emphasizing relationships has led to what we might expect now that we know about Radical Connection: more transactional forms of fundraising, prioritizing wealth over engagement. That's because nonprofits looked at donor prospects for what they are worth, not how much they aligned with their organization or tribe. Sidenote: It is encouraging that some people gave to specific nonprofits for the first time during the pandemic. For instance, Feeding America, a national network of more than 200 food banks, raised more than $515 million in 2020. According to The Chronicle of Philanthropy this is "more than three-and-a-half times what it did in 2019."

Still, many ongoing relationships were ignored. Or at least not well-nurtured. By now, it should be clear that the main problem with transactional giving is its *transitory nature*. Think about what usually happens when a hurricane or natural disaster strikes. The crisis makes the news, spurring donations for a (limited) time when the tragedy is still fresh in the public consciousness. Yet, when the emergency vanishes from awareness, so does the outpouring. Giving tends to stop as people move on to the next thing, unaware their ongoing support is needed to tackle other humanitarian needs.

THE REACHING YOUNG PEOPLE QUANDARY

Returning to the Kaplans' story to illustrate the bigger picture, it's doubtful today's teens or 20-somethings might romantically meet at a gala like Irving and Barbara did. Instead, they're more likely to cross paths online. *Statista* reports 30 million people now use web dating services, with this figure likely to reach 35 million by 2024. Also, according to Pew Research, nearly half of 18- to 29-year-olds say they have used a dating app. Remembering how malls, once bastions of hangout coolness, have emptied, replaced by screen interactions—even before COVID-19—it remains to be seen how today's youth will establish their own future social traditions. Twenty years from now, will a future Irving encourage his kids to join an organization like City of Hope that meant so much to him growing up? Likewise, will a future Barbara tell her children to volunteer for Habitat for Humanity or some similar group because it meant a lot to her, keeping in their family's tradition? These are big unknowns.

What we can say is today's youth are not growing up in a world emphasizing in-person relationships or social skills so critical for Radical Connection. In 2017, *Men's Health* suggested the art of conversation is dying for most people in America. "In fact, 65 percent of millennials don't feel confident in face-to-face social interactions, a new One Poll survey of 2,000 young Americans (18 or older) found. The survey, commissioned by Don Pablo Coffee, also discovered that 30 percent of millennials cancel or just don't go to events they're invited to because they fear it will be socially awkward."

If we no longer live in a culture of conversation leading to trust, how can we expect young people to develop long-term relationships with nonprofits? The answer is we can't. Worse, when it comes to the Generosity Crisis, we know transactional giving, the type often reinforced by many nonprofits, leads to reduced donor retention. Writing for *NonProfitPro* in June 2021, analyst Steve McLaughlin recently highlighted this truth in a revealing piece on retention. Based on data from Blackbaud Target Analytics, we can assume that if 100 new donors gifted an organization via traditional offline channels (via mail, the phone, in-person events, or any interaction not involving the web), we could expect a 29% retention rate. "Meaning that of those 100 new donors that gave to your organization, there are only 29 left one year later. Not good," writes McLaughlin. "Second, let's assume that all of those 100 new donors gave a gift to your organization online, through a website or on a mobile device. Sadly, the first year, online-acquired retention rate for these donors is even worse. A year later, you would only have 22 of the 100 new donors that you were given. Really not good."

Sadly, the financial goal of many nonprofits is attaining an annual fundraising revenue target goal rather than focusing on growing donors to support the organization year over year. The failure to engage, thank, communicate, connect, and foster relationships causes nonprofits to spend contributed dollars and energy to continue the vicious cycle of finding and converting new donors, rather than engaging and retaining existing supporters. They are not realizing the gains available for Radical Connection.

Yet even McLaughlin's sobering retention statistics and so much evidence of millennials' deteriorating social skills fail to fully apprehend the danger of our crisis. What we left out so far is the *cultural impact* of a generation uninitiated in generosity's virtues. From previous chapters, we know religious institutions play a big role in promoting such values. But fewer young people now identify as religious, diminishing spirituality's power to influence their thinking and behavior. As Public Religion Research Institute reported in 2020, "The increase in proportion of religiously unaffiliated Americans has occurred across all age groups but has been most pronounced among young Americans. In 1986, only 10% of those ages 18–29 identified as religiously unaffiliated. In 2016, that number had increased to 38%, and declined slightly in 2020, to 36%."

Faith's importance in generosity should not go unnoticed in this discussion. According to the 2017 GUSA Special Report, "People who are religiously affiliated are more likely to make a charitable donation of any kind, whether to a religious congregation or to another type of charitable organization. Sixty-two percent of religious households give to charity of any kind, compared with 46 percent of households with no religious affiliation." Equally as important, households with a religious affiliation give twice as much as those that don't, essentially doubling a person's "generosity quotient."

A HYBRID SOLUTION IN SIGHT?

Some of us would rather return to a simpler time, an era in which the Kaplans met and fell in love IRL. But the genie has left the bottle. Unless something massive like a solar flare knocks out the electric grid anytime soon, we're unlikely to technologically regress in the coming years. Rather than wring our hands at the misfortune of it all, let's do something about it. How? First, let's recall our central thesis: Solving the Generosity Crisis requires greater human connection. Knowing that cultivating deeper relationships must be our North Star for positive change, we must turn to tech to facilitate more community-building activities, both on and offline. Before we do, let's consider the mechanics involved in this paradigm shift. Then we'll offer a case study highlighting one of the most interesting ways this could come together.

LEVERAGING TECH FOR GOOD

Contrary to conventional messaging for innovation suggesting it's a force for division, it's *already* being used to develop deeper relationships. As discussed in Chapter 7, Nathan's work since 2017 has been focused on harnessing the latest deep-learning algorithms, along with big data, to engage donor prospects based on not just their wealth but on their depth of *connection* to a cause or a nonprofit. From Donor-Search's website: "We help prospect researchers and gift officers connect with people who have an affinity for your cause by providing insights into the giving history of donors who are likely to give to you. Our philanthropy-first focus helps nonprofits focus on the relationships that will last and grow with your organization."

Now, let's look at one of the largest health-care systems in the US to understand this approach. When Nathan began consulting with them several years ago, they were stuck in a fundraising model that unfortunately is all too common. They employed two approaches:

- **Spray and pray:** Also considered the "shotgun approach," it involves mass mailing appeal letters to various zip codes to secure donations.

- **Targeting rich prospects:** Using wealth data, like real estate holdings and SEC filings, they focused disproportionately on individuals with high net worth, rather than gauging a person's engagement with a hospital.

Was their strategy working? Not really. As discussed, contrary to what many think, wealth and giving aren't directly correlated. Instead, as Donor Loyalty Study conducted by Abila, reports, "The three main reasons people donate to nonprofit organizations are very personal in nature—they have a deep passion for the cause, they believe the organization depends on their donation, or they know someone affected by the nonprofit's mission."

Informed by this insight, Nathan used a different approach. Through deep learning, Nathan and his team proved a person's wealth was helpful in determining how much someone might give, but only 10% correlated to whether the person was *altruistic*. Nathan therefore suggested his client turn to those key indicators likely to suggest a patient's connection with the hospital. Here are some relevant data points:

- Volunteerism levels

- Attendance at events

- Email open rate and online engagement

- Interactions with specific clinicians and departments

Nathan and his team enriched this content with public information such as what other charities prospects give to, their political/religious affiliations, even the magazines they read, and so on to generate insights based on more than 1,000 data points. Afterwards, they used AI to determine commonalities between donors and non-donors. Then they scored every constituent based on their model. The resulting score was displayed in a simple visualization tool helping gift officers to more easily identify individuals with the highest potential to take a prospective meeting.

What Nathan offered could be considered the more *digital* component of a hospital's fundraising strategy. Old-school outreach was the analog part. The organization's leaders and its gift officers used insights provided by Nathan to target preselected individuals to solicit donations. Prospecting in this manner provides a more holistic and more donor-centric approach to first identify people who are engaged and likely to engage with the organization based on their past experiences versus their wealth. Did it work? Yes! It led to the organization's best fundraising year. *Ever*.

Here are the statistics:

- It raised $66 million in 2021 alone, more than 6% over the prior year.

- 5,500 people gave for the first time.

- The average gift increased from $110 to $150 per person.

For those that know Nathan, this result wasn't such a shocker. He's often said that the ideal fundraising should center on someone's wealth never settled well with him. Knowing instead how most people give based on their experiences with an organization is really the key. The real surprise? This hospital client experienced a record-breaking fundraising year during the pandemic—at a time when so many hospitals were cutting budgets, people were losing their jobs, and in-person fundraising events were canceled.

GENEROSITY'S FUTURE

As shown in previous chapters, Nathan and the DonorSearch team are revolutionizing fundraising by shifting the focus from purely looking at the wealth of prospects to measuring who is radically connected to an organization. Their unique approach requires proprietary technology and a group of the world's leading experts. Although most nonprofits could greatly benefit from partnering with DonorSearch, there are a range of technologies that don't require proprietary tech to start using today—and these technologies are critical to the future of generosity. A more thorough discussion of these exciting innovations may be found in the 2022 book *The Smart Nonprofit: Staying Human-Centered in an Automated World* by Beth Kanter and Allison H. Fine. Here's a brief description: "*The Smart Nonprofit* offers a road map for the once-in-a-generation opportunity to remake work and accelerate positive social change. It comes from understanding how to use smart tech strategically, ethically, and well."

So far, we have indicated tech tools of the *Smart Nonprofit* variety can marry the digital world with the analog to target the right prospects in real time and better connect with them, but we still haven't solved the relationship quandary or the reaching young people quandary.

So, what is the right tech strategy to solve these challenges? *The metaverse.* For those unfamiliar with this concept, the term comes from author Neal Stephenson's 1992 novel *Snow Crash* as a virtual reality-based successor to the internet (though the book predates widespread public usage). The 2011 novel *Ready Player One*—later adapted to the Steven Spielberg–directed film—also offers an exploration of this concept. Both stories depict a not-so-distant future in which online spaces have gone three-dimensional, offering an immersive experience combining virtual and augmented reality to approximate the feeling one is ensconced inside cyberspace.

Seems far-fetched, right?

It did for much of the public until CEO Mark Zuckerberg announced he was changing Facebook's name to Meta, reflecting his social media empire's pivot. "Today we're seen as a social media company," he said on October 28, 2021, in an announcement. "But in our DNA, we are a company that builds technology to connect people. And the metaverse is the next frontier just like social networking was when we got started." (Zuckerberg admitted he chose the name *Meta* because of its Greek etymology. It means "beyond." To this point, he added, "For me, it symbolizes that there is always more to build.")

THE KAPLANS 2.0?

In the spirit of going beyond, it's time for another story, a sequel of sorts to the Kaplans. We will imagine a future in which non-profits harness tech in novel ways, producing Radical Connection. Our tale begins with Simon, a 20-something entrepreneur who lives and works in Palo Alto, California. A coding savant, Simon declined a job offer from Google before dropping out of high school. He and three friends launched several startups, solving problems from detecting wire fraud to enabling tokenized real estate investment.

On the other side of the country lives Claudine, another entrepreneur. Also in her late 20s, she made her fortune as the proprietor of clothing boutiques in downtown Atlanta. Like Simon, Claudine also dropped out of high school but for different reasons. Claudine suffered from a toxic upbringing. For years, her stepfather made untoward overtures. By the time she was 17, Claudine had had enough and left home permanently. The first place she worked was for a thrift shop where she learned the business. Fast. Before age 20, she owned her own store. By 25, she operated 10 more and was a millionaire.

Simon and Claudine have never met or heard of each other. Though neither knows it, they are bound by their devotion to doing good. Financial supporters of CARE, they each donate substantially to the nonprofit dedicated to defeating poverty for "the world's most vulnerable people." CARE and the Mastercard Center for Inclusive Growth partnered in the form of CARE's Ignite Program. Intended to reach 3.9 million fledgling entrepreneurs in Peru, Pakistan, and Vietnam, the initiative "opens up much-needed access to finance, technology, and networks and builds entrepreneurship capacity and skills." Meant to raise the standards of living for workers, families, and their communities, it's geared to women-owned or -operated endeavors. "Locally, CARE partners with financial service providers, helping them to adapt existing products and services supporting micro and small businesses."

On opposite sides of the country, Simon and Claudine happen to be contributing money and mentorship to a Vietnamese woman named Huong. Both were touched to see the video application the 18-year-old shot on her phone depicting the poverty she and her family endure in Saigon. Simon got teary seeing the cramped shack housing Huong, her parents, and her little sister, who was born with a rare disease that prevented her from walking normally and controlling her bladder. Likewise, Claudine got goosebumps as Huong described her dream in broken English, "I want to build my own store—place where people buy clothes and feel good."

Simon and Claudine also know investing in Huong will help Huong's family and her community. Proponents of the idea that a rising tide lifts all ships, they envision an emergent phenomenon whereby more entrepreneurs and locals benefit from increased trade and business opportunities. They are not alone. A slew of philanthropists from around the world also donate to Huong, serving as virtual mentors during frequent Zoom check-in calls.

It's during one of these videoconferences that Claudine notices Simon. She thinks he's cute and likes the way he patiently explains the more technical aspects of Huong's backend operations. A year later she gets a chance to "meet" him when some of the most passionate CARE supporters go on site visits to chat with local entrepreneurs. Both Simon and Claudine have been invited to see how Huong has fared since receiving their support. Only, there's a twist to this arrangement. They are going to meet with her entirely virtually. They are not alone. A dozen such supporters also virtually attend the launch of Huong's boutique.

What makes her store so unusual is it straddles the virtual and real world. Located at a busy Saigon intersection, the physical location offers walk-in customers a chance to sift through clothing racks for local-sourced apparel. At the same time, a nearly identical facsimile of the store exists in the metaverse, available to customers no matter where they happen to be.

Despite all his coding prowess, Simon was inexperienced with VR until now. His skintight haptic suit provided by CARE confused him the first time he put it on. He found it funny to wear, like being dipped in chocolate it was so form-fitting. But his concerns vanished when he jacked into the metaverse and discovered how haptics can convince you that you really are somewhere else.

As E. Bruce Goldstein explains in an *Encyclopedia of Perception*, "Haptic technology does for the sense of touch what computer graphics does for vision. Haptic technology allows creating computer-generated Haptic Virtual Objects (HVOs), which can be touched and manipulated with one's hands or body. HVOs provide a rich combination of cutaneous and kinesthetic stimulation through a bidirectional haptic (touch) information flow between HVOs and human users."

The moment Simon "left" his home in Palo Alto for Vietnam, the physical world lost its grip. Instead, he feasted on sensory delights in the metaverse. Beside the Saigon River with its swampland ringed with foliage rose a phalanx of slab-like high-rises. He felt the sun's warmth on his skin as a faint breeze whispered by. All around he heard honking horns on choked city streets and voices from scattered conversations throughout the market. Turning his head, he saw a sign reading *Vẻ đẹp*—meaning beautiful in Vietnamese—atop the cream-colored boutique entrance. Presenting a modern façade, Simon marveled at its clean, elegant exterior. Huong's creation could easily stand up to the understated elegance of any shop on Bond Street. Hearing the tinkle of a bell as he entered the premises, Simon drank in the small but inviting clothing exchange. Some of his fellow CARE donors were also present, already browsing virtual racks. He didn't notice the one person more interested in looking at him than the merchandise.

Approaching a rack, Simon absently ran his fingers along the soft silk of a chiffon blouse. Even though he helped design this simulacrum of the real *Vẻ đẹp* existing on the other side of the globe, he chuckled to himself at its seeming physicality, its ability to trick his senses. He recalled Huong's insistence that she create *two* emporiums, one virtual, one real, the latter so she could go up against those deep-pocketed local competitors able to afford a larger brick-and-mortar location.

*****

On the other side of the room, as Claudine watched Simon, she prepared her opening lines. *Nice to meet you—in the metaverse.* Or *fancy meeting* you *here.* None of them passed muster. An introvert by nature, she talked herself out of approaching the cute techie. Instead, she stumbled into a conversation with nearby donors about how Huong is already aiding other local entrepreneurs by acquiring, then reselling their clothing and shoes.

"And I heard her family can finally move into a bigger place," said one.

"And her sister's getting better medical treatment," another puts in.

Claudine moved on to a hallway where she noticed a framed picture of a crisp-looking Oxford shirt. As she drew nearer, what she saw expanded. She now glimpsed *many* beautiful men's shirts and not all of them white. She looked around, realizing she was no longer even in the same hallway. Somehow, by investigating the frame more closely, she had transported into another show-room of sorts. Whistling to herself, she admired what Simon and the software engineers had accomplished. Whereas a typical second-hand retailer might have but *one* type of shirt based on size, design, and especially availability, Huong's boutique didn't suffer the same restraints. Virtual customers could access a vast selection of apparel, some of which could be ordered on demand, bypassing analog inventory and space considerations.

"Now, this was a great idea," she heard a woman say.

Turning, Claudine saw it was Huong speaking to Simon. The young woman was taking him on a virtual showroom tour through immersive displays. She stopped to watch as Simon slipped on a navy-blue blazer. Claudine couldn't help imagining him wearing it on a date with her.

*****

A few weeks before the site visit, Simon received a package containing ingredients for Vietnamese pho. It contained precut thin brisket strips, flat rice noodles, beef broth, and a splash of fish sauce. Like other attendees, he received instructions to prepare the meal at home before joining the virtual gala. Simon did as he was told. Though not an experienced chef, he felt proud his soup came out quite flavorful. As it steamed in a bowl beside his complimentary chopsticks, Simon suited back up, reentering the metaverse.

This time, he found himself in an elegant ballroom. A full orchestra played ska-influenced Glenn Miller standards.

Charming flower arrangements matched the polished silver-
ware at large round tables seating up to six. Beforehand Simon
had picked out his look. He wore a dark tuxedo with a simple
black tie and white shirt. Not everyone chose to be so traditional, he noticed. One man picked John Travolta's white suit
from *Saturday Night Fever*. A female selected a robe and cape
straight of Hogwarts.

The evening's festivities included a speech from Huong in
which she thanked attendees for their generosity. Joined onstage
with her family, she told everyone how her dreams were coming
true—thanks to them. Simon ate his pho at home while clapping
along, marveling at the uncanniness of merging his immediate
surroundings with this convincing virtual reality. When the program ended, Simon had an urge to do what he usually did at the
galas he attended IRL: go home. He wasn't a schmoozer at heart.

As he prepared to log off, he felt a tap on his shoulder.
Turning, he saw Claudine, one of the donors from the Zoom
calls. For a second, he was speechless. She looked radiant in a
long green gown; her brown locks curled down to her bare
shoulders.

"Want to dance?" she asked as the band launched into
In the Mood.

In real life, Simon might have been too shy to say yes—the
last time he tried dancing was a disastrous prom date—but participating virtually felt safer somehow. He grasped Claudine's
arm in his, entering the dance floor. Taking their place beside
other couples, he and Claudine swayed to the music.

"You've done this before," Claudine smiled.

"Not really. And never in cyberspace."

"Me neither. But it's sure fun."

Simon forgot himself. Drinking in Claudine's perfume and buoyed by the live orchestra, he twirled her around the floor. Smiling, she kept up with his footwork, lost in the moment. When the song ended, Simon surprised them both by dipping her backwards to applause.

"Aren't you going to kiss me?" Claudine looked up at him.

Before the year ended, this encounter became fodder for wedding toasts to the happy bride and groom. In time, they would repeat its particulars to their three kids as the story of how mom and dad came together.

Growing up hearing this story had another lasting impact. Their children—then later, their children's children—were so affected by this tale, they embraced the giving tradition, making generosity part of their family's identity, paying forward kindness. Like a ripple in a pond, such benevolence spread to others, influencing generations to come, even if centuries from now, no one could pinpoint precisely where such benevolent feelings originated.

WHAT THE NEW KAPLANS CAN TEACH US

Too many people operate under the belief nonprofits remain 15 to 30 years behind the business world. But as statesman Winston Churchill once remarked, "Never let a good crisis go to waste." In the spirit of innovation and goodwill to humankind, let's seize this moment to not just tell a new story about philanthropy but to bring real change to fruition. Tech such as the metaverse, along with other advancements such as AI and big data, needn't act as barriers to greater interpersonal connection. Instead, they can be harnessed to develop stronger relationships and spark more young people's interest in giving.

Even better, thinking outside the box when it comes to connectivity can solve other problems. Consider how groups like Charity: Water often fly their biggest donors to far-flung locales to observe the work they are doing, such as well-digging. This is, of course, costly, not to mention that it presents environmental concerns. Not only that, but international travel can also put donors at risk. Nathan's father-in-law was a doctor who volunteered with the World Health Organization for decades to help end polio and would often journey to developing countries. He was mugged in Afghanistan and Brazil while on polio surveillance assignments. What dangers might he have avoided if there were other innovative ways to help? But mitigating hazards is only *one* reason to leverage innovation for Radical Connection. Others come into focus if we expand our thinking.

Imagine a future where the following could happen:

- Lifesaving robotic surgeries take place on different continents.

- Special Olympics competitions draw more global participants.

- Donors can watch—and help build homes—from their living rooms.

These examples just scratch the surface as to what's possible when we think differently about generosity. Determining how future efforts are imagined and brought to life will make for important discussion topics in the coming years. For now, what matters is we understand what's at stake, and what's doable when we open our minds. Truly, marrying the old and the new offers tomorrow's nonprofits a fighting chance to solve our Generosity Crisis at last.

*****

For now, it's our sincerest hope that reading this book has helped you to think (or rethink) your own connections to organizations wishing to do good. We began our discussion with a dramatic representation of our crisis on purpose. This was to shake up your worldview, to disrupt you. To show you that a looming disaster exists you may not even be aware of. Or ever contemplated. Now that you better understand the problem before us, we encourage you to create dialogue with others. If you are involved with a nonprofit, help others to see how they can connect the mission with those donors and volunteers they wish to reach. If you're not aligned with a cause, take that step today. Not only will the world be a better place because of your efforts but also you will personally benefit from your new Radical Connection in so many ways. After all, it's the human relationships that bring about the best philanthropic results, leading to increased giving and better outcomes for humanity at large.

Likewise, if you are a parent or in a position of authority, we ask that you please share these principles with your family or those you lead. It's not enough that *you* better appreciate the tremendous challenges we face. The next generation must fully understand the virtues of giving and what humanity stands to lose should it cease. Accordingly, we ask that you lead by example, modeling to others the responsibility—and privilege—of giving back, but more importantly, the value others stand to receive when participating in this critical work.

For those in the nonprofit sector, we hope this book opened your eyes to the fact that what's working today won't necessarily continue in the future. Left unchecked, our Generosity Crisis will not solve itself. Instead, it will metastasize, harming society, undoing so many great works and cultural mainstays we now take for granted. We especially hope our discussion enabled you to contemplate the differences between transactional and Radical Connection—and how to foster the latter. If you come from the corporate side, humanity is riding on your commitment to get involved through innovative approaches and novel partnerships to scale social good. Empowered with this knowledge, no matter your background and expertise, you will shape tomorrow—so make it count. All it takes is strengthening your relationships with others so they possess stronger rapport, deeper connection, and greater love toward humankind.

Last, it's *still* not enough to know these things rationally. Action is required. Every day you have the chance to improve things, to help your fellow citizen and our planet. Don't just read these words and return to your screens. Get involved. Pay it forward. Deliver that sandwich. Volunteer at your school or church. Build that house. Give that shirt off your back. No matter what—just make a difference. We're counting on you. Let's do this together.

*****

In our next and final chapter, we will present interviews with cutting-edge leaders of nonprofit organizations and for-profit corporations who are walking the walk when it comes to adapting to changes in the philanthropic landscape. They're leading the charge for Radical Connection to amazing results. Their experiences show us what's possible when we transform our great crisis into our great opportunity.

CHAPTER **10**

Notes from the Field
Interviews with Tomorrow's Generosity Leaders

Philanthropy's future is no abstract discussion. Already, non-profits and corporations with a strong CSR mission are using tech to change its course—*even as we write this book*. In our final chapter, we present discussions with cutting-edge organizations blazing new, exciting paths. Each example shows us how to restore generosity to its rightful place of importance before it's too late. Although these entities are diverse in nature, they are united in one key area—their desire to improve the world, beginning with a drive toward Radical Connection using both precision and personalization.

THE FARMLINK PROJECT: CHALLENGING THE STATUS QUO

Not every nonprofit has been around for decades. The Farmlink Project was begun, just as COVID-19 gripped the world, by an unsuspecting but passionate group college students unwilling to sit back and watch people struggle with food insecurity. The youthfulness and entrepreneurism of driven college students has manifested a no-holds-barred commitment to doing whatever it takes in the moment. Unrestricted by bureaucracy or "the way we've always done it" mentality, the culture of The Farmlink Project team is to act swiftly in the greatest time of need. This up-and-coming organization is a prime example of how the right people, driven by passion and innovation, can tackle an important and monumental mission *immediately* by inviting others in partnership by connecting passion with purpose.

Farmlink Project's ambitious goal is to feed people in need by connecting farmers with surplus crops and those individuals most needing nourishment.

It launched after the founders saw two separate phenomenon that might not have seem connected initially but led to their "eureka" moment. First, as the pandemic raged, food banks around the nation reported shortages as more Americans needed support feeding their families. At the same time, farmers had to dump millions of pounds of critical products such as eggs, potatoes, and milk due to supply chain problems. Farmlink swooped in with a vision: solve both challenges by facilitating the transport of surplus crops to food banks.

Even before its formal legal creation as a 501(c)(3) nonprofit organization, the small army of college student volunteers managed a major feat: moving a million pounds of food, staving off needless waste and hunger. Its concept successfully proven, Farmlink was off to the races. From its founding through early 2022, the organization has saved 77 million pounds of food (that's 64 million meals!) that would have otherwise been disposed of due to the endemic food surplus crisis, exasperated by COVID-19. To date, just 24 months after moving its first truck of surplus eggs from a California farm to a local foodbank, Farmlink's efforts have resulted in more than 58 million meals served to those in need while also generating $4.1 million in economic relief to farmers and truckers. The burgeoning nonprofit has already provided food to 266 underserved communities across 48 states. What follows is our interview with founding members of The Farmlink Project: James Kanoff, Aidan Reilly, and Ben Collier.

How has tech helped you reach partners, employees, and volunteers?

We would have struggled to launch The Farmlink Project even six months before we did if not for emerging resources. Our organization is built entirely upon remote working tools like Slack, Zoom, and other software applications. All at once, the whole world became familiar with these innovations, enabling distanced work and education. This helped both our employees and volunteers to feel natural working in this manner. Also, we used social media and other online marketing to reach the public because that's how our team resonates with messaging ourselves.

Still, one of our biggest challenges continues to be how to better use tech to ensure our online outreach works as well as it can. Already, we utilize algorithms and machine learning to help us understand what best connects with different community segments on different platforms at different times. For our first 18 months, it felt like we were throwing a dart from outer space, hoping to hit that social media bull's-eye. Now we can be much more precise.

The data has been eye-opening. For example, a picture we used in a marketing campaign resonated with our audience six months ago. Now it doesn't have the same effect. In the past we might have kept using it. Now we know to reframe. Critically, we don't use this technology to build the narratives we want to share. Instead, we've always relied on a simple message that clearly communicates our mission and how we wish to accomplish it. The difference is that our machine learning algorithms allow us to be much more precise and effective in targeting that message.

Why do relationships matter so much when fighting hunger?

We work with three different groups to combat food insecurity:

- Farmers with surplus crops

- Food banks in need of nourishing meals
- Truckers who move the food

Now, logistics companies are typically tech-savvy, but food banks and farmers are more *relationship driven*. From the outset, our job was to counter the distrust many farmers and food banks might have held had for an upstart composed of young people. We did this by forming relationships, doing what we said we would do, and proving our model works. This built trust.

While innovation has massively helped connect volunteers and donors in our community, we couldn't use it the same way to connect with critical partners to Farmlink, both on the farms and in the food banks. We forged those relationships through old-fashioned communication. Even so, tech facilitated this work because we could offload so many admin tasks off to computer systems, allowing us to concentrate on relationship building. We began with a lot of cold calling, convincing hard-working, honest people dedicated to food growing and distribution we weren't a scam. Nowadays, having proven what we can do, we have farmers and food banks calling *us* to join the program. This is the result of building relationships from the start.

How do you see the ways you connect with others as more than just transactional?

As a new organization, some of our best successes in getting people involved were transactional, initially. For example, our largest fundraising campaign to date is with Chipotle. Customers can round up their bill by adding a small donation to our cause. This raised an astonishing $1.1 million. Another similar initiative with Chipotle funded transport of 300,000 pounds of food last year—all by adding a code to online orders.

Nonetheless, we believe it's important to take these relationships that began with a transaction and turn them into something deeper. We are exploring many ways to do this. First, we are creating messaging to share the story of the communities our donors help, like reports from New Mexico's Navajo Nation where we distributed 40,000 pounds of food.

These types of success stories remind our community that it's not just about pounds of food moved. It's the *people* that food feeds. Next, we're harnessing tech to create deeper connections to The Farmlink Project. Last year we began accepting cryptocurrency donations. This was a big hit with our younger audience. We are also exploring NFTs and working with VR to provide donors with a firsthand experience of a farm or a food bank we partner with. Many donors, like millions of Chipotle patrons, have never been on a farm and are fortunate enough to have never visited a food pantry. Bringing them to these locations virtually enables deeper connections, fostering a mutual drive to end hunger in America.

What can nonprofits do to ensure the future of philanthropy?

Everyone on our team grew up with a tradition of giving in their families. We took it for granted that America is the most generous country on earth and always will be. We've only just begun and will continue to challenge the status quo. We see the challenge of connecting people with our project and will continue to take risks and to innovate new ways of fostering connection. We can regain control of our destiny by fostering those deep connections that turn one-time donors into lifetime supporters. Even as a new organization, we've witnessed this victory firsthand as volunteers became true believers upon delivering their first truck full of farm-fresh produce. It mirrors our own transformation: how many of us also became true believers delivering our first truckload. If we can create this deep connection, every nonprofit in America can, too, if only they communicate in the right way to the right people.

*****

For a group of college students who weren't content sitting in their dorms waiting for the "adults to take care of it," The Farmlink Project team has accomplished more in the first two years of its existence than many nonprofits accomplish in their lifetimes. This is a story of hope: hope for a future generation of mission-driven leaders who aren't content with the idea of maintaining the status quo but rather act by connecting people with authenticity and passion.

ILLUMINA: THE TRIPLE BOTTOM LINE MEETS NEXT-GEN GENETICISTS

Many companies are engaged in solving puzzles of one sort or another, but Illumina focuses on the ultimate puzzle—the genome. Illumina develops and manufactures genomic sequencers, microarrays, and analysis technologies that enable its customers to power their applications in basic research, agriculture, metagenomics, translational medicine, and clinical testing. Its technologies can help to decode what each person's unique genome says about their health and other attributes. It also unlocks future medical innovations. Illumina has a strong culture of corporate social responsibility, expressed in its approach to business and the Illumina Corporate Foundation, offering key charitable grants to nonprofits.

Equally driven to innovate, by 2014, Illumina had lowered the cost of sequencing the human genome from $1 million (in 2007) to just $1,000, making it more reasonable expenditure for much of the world. One of the company's goals is to lower this cost even further to just $100. It has reached $600 as of 2022. Meanwhile, Illumina donated $14.5 million in 2021, supporting 1,345 causes. It also continues to reach more than 315,000 STEM learners with critical education programs. The authors were pleased to sit down with Tiana Austel, senior specialist of the corporate social responsibility team at Illumina, to learn more about the company's approach to CSR.

Do you have a "why"?

Our CSR mission is "Deepening our impact on human health by serving as a champion for patients, our communities, our people, and our planet." We apply this reason for being to key areas as part of our overall CSR strategy.

Here's what we are doing in practice:

- **Expanding access:** By driving down the price of genomics, we expand testing availability and improve data diversity. Both promise transformative, positive effects for medicine.

- **Empowering our communities:** Via grants and sharing our time, talents, and technology, we support patients and next generation geneticists.

- **Integrating environmental sustainability:** Committed to environmental stewardship, we work tirelessly to protect and preserve our planet.

- **Nurturing our people:** We foster a culture of care fueled by supporting one another, promoting collaboration, inspiring innovation, and fostering diversity, equity, and inclusion.

- **Operate responsibly:** As a genomics pioneer, we ensure the technology we create and the data we collect are used safely, ethically, and responsibly.

What is your proudest accomplishment?

One of our most memorable successes has been "The Future is Bright." An educational program designed to expose schoolchildren to genomics, it offers hands-on activities and access to STEM professionals in our company. They answer questions and provide career advice to tomorrow's scientists. The Future is Bright came together because a small group within Illumina had an honest conversation about the state of STEM education during the COVID-19 pandemic. We realized students of all ages were receiving little hands-on science education. Believing we possessed the capability to interest future scientists, we got to work designing a program just for them.

In only three months, we put together curriculum and classroom materials, including a kit to extract the DNA of strawberries. We also established infrastructure to host video calls between professionals within Illumina and classes of students. We set a goal of involving 10,000 children in the program but ended up with an incredible 40,000 participants. We also set a goal of 50,000 for year two, but actually achieved participation of 90,000. At the same time, program involvement within Illumina expanded significantly. Most notably, we went from three participants at the senior management and above level to 37—including the CTO. The Future is Bright has been a huge success, and we expect significant growth in year three.

Who do you help and what is the challenge they face?

Helping *all* of humanity is the focus of our genetics work, both from a corporate CSR perspective and that of the Illumina Corporate Foundation. If we zero in on The Future is Bright program, our immediate emphasis is on America's schoolchildren.

As mentioned, the challenge they face is a lack of hands-on science experiments. Simply extracting DNA from a strawberry generates a connection to STEM that no number of lectures or YouTube videos can possibly create. Unfortunately, many students often have no access to STEM professionals beyond teachers. By connecting with diverse Illumina employees who work in cutting-edge science, students of all backgrounds, especially young women and minority students, can see firsthand that people just like them are improving humankind working in STEM.

The Future is Bright not only helps children enjoy a hands-on lesson in DNA but also the program has been a benefit to our employees, especially those who are younger and believe one's career needs to be a *calling*. Our staff at all levels have been energized by hosting video calls with young people asking questions about what Illumina does and how DNA sequencing helps others. It's become part of our talent acquisition program as more prospects share concern about the triple bottom line. We regularly hear from recruiters asking, "What exciting CSR programs do we have cooking?" There's a sense we are in a new era in which companies need to give back in their communities—a challenge corporate America is just waking up to.

How can technology connect people in a more personal way?

Innovation is critical to building and maintaining personal connections as projects scale. For instance, a small team on our side launched The Future is Bright using basic tools, yet by year two, recent advancements vastly improved how we operated the program. Interestingly, the solutions we found weren't new systems, but rather the application of extant tools Illumina uses for business, now retooled for unique opportunities.

The technology that made the difference was a site allowing us to automatically connect teachers with members of the Illumina team. Instead of contacting a nameless, faceless corporation, teachers were instead put directly in contact with an expert automatically, instead of relying on our team to make an assignment. Personalization at scale like this is only possible with technology in our experience. When it frees up a percentage of our day, that newly available time allows us to tackle more worthy tasks—which is good as there's never a shortage of work to do in the CSR world.

How do you view philanthropy's future?

When we talk about tomorrow, the idea that really resonates with us is being precise and strategic in our impact. Precision via personalized connections ensures our efforts are creating positive results, and maintaining a strategic vision ensures our projects and grants are aligned with our mission. Finally, we believe CSR efforts will continue to become more integrated with other business units so that product teams and others can work synergistically. Our work cannot be done without buy-in throughout the company. Conversely, making meaningful contributions in our communities benefits our company in many ways, including talent recruitment. Creating a symbiotic relationship across the company's operations and our CSR initiatives will ensure a healthy, robust future for the work we do.

THE RASKOB FOUNDATION: KEEPING MORE GENERATIONS INVOLVED IN TRADITION

Both tourists and New Yorkers alike acknowledge the Empire State Building is the most iconic landmark in the Big Apple. Yes, there are taller buildings in Manhattan, but nothing symbolizes the heart of New York City quite like the famous edifice. It remains one of the most recognizable buildings in America—and not just because of its starring role in *King Kong* action flicks.

Still, there are interesting tidbits about it you might not know. For one thing, the Empire State Building was built just before the Great Depression. Not exactly the best time to be in the commercial real estate business! Seen at this time as an expensive boondoggle, critics derided it as the "Empty State Building." However, it wasn't long before it gained its legendary status in American culture. Even so, it wouldn't exist today if not for the extraordinary vision and determination of one man—financier John Raskob.

Raskob wasn't just responsible for the erection of one of our most famous landmarks. He also pioneered the concept of consumer credit at General Motors, developing what later became GMAC to provide regular working Americans with loans to buy cars they might otherwise never afford. The Empire State Building is part of Raskob's enduring legacy, but toward the end of his life, he established a very different sort of legacy with his wife, The Raskob Foundation for Catholic Activities.

Helena S. "Skipper" Raskob once said, "When building, build forever." Truer words were never spoken about the Raskob Foundation. Since 1945, the nonprofit has donated more than $200 million to worthy causes related to the Catholic faith. Recent grants include replacing the heating system at a nursing home, funding a Connecticut program to help renters facing eviction, and funding a Florida camp serving children and adults with disabilities.

The Raskob Foundation currently involves more than 80 members of the extended family, with three generations of relatives participating in the organization. We sat down with Patrick McGrory, chairperson of the Raskob Foundation, to learn more about the challenges and benefits of a family foundation—and tradition—in today's unprecedented giving climate.

On learning about generosity at a young age

Patrick explained to us that even as a child he knew something special was going on whenever he would attend family gatherings. Unlike some families, his extended relatives got together for something bigger than just holidays or birthdays. As a 10-year-old, Patrick recognized that the get-togethers in Wilmington, Delaware, served a higher purpose. It wasn't more than a few years later that he was introduced to the family legacy of giving.

As noted throughout this book, generosity used to be a tradition handed down from generation to generation, but this observance is on the decline.

Not so much for the Raskobs, fortunately. Patrick explains his first exposure to the family foundation, saying, "Around 13 or so, I started attending formal meetings with my mom. The many gatherings and the interactions served to provide a surround sound of giving that became embedded in me."

These meetings imprinted generosity onto Patrick's character, so much so that giving continually occupied his mind, whether he was at a family function or not. He recalls that his grandfather and grandmother weren't involved in the foundation because the former served as a judge, yet throughout their lives both were quietly generous, giving to causes without fanfare. During their lifetimes the Generosity Crisis was already brewing, but it didn't sway the Raskob family. According to Patrick, the close-knit nature of the foundation, plus his family's legacy of giving, ensured their characteristic generosity passed from generation to generation. Continuing this family trait remains of prime importance to Patrick.

The challenges of passing generosity on

Patrick spends significant time contemplating the Raskob Foundation's future. Currently, most of the board of trustees is composed of fifth- and sixth-generation Raskobs. Continuing the family's legacy of giving through to the seventh generation in our rapidly changing world remains his priority. His own educational pursuits very much contribute to his strategy as chairperson.

Patrick is currently working on a Ph.D. with his dissertation centered on building efficiencies into family foundations during generational change. His research into philanthropy reinforces much of what we've documented in this book, especially the difference between transactional connections and Radical Connections. As Patrick says, "It's clear there is a *continuum* of philanthropy, providing various levels of which you can be engaged with giving back. Those levels range from the basic activities (often facilitated via social media/internet activities) to the more fully involved experiences, including volunteering, interacting, discussing challenges, and seeking novel opportunities. It is obvious that different levels of philanthropic engagement impact you personally, and ultimately, the world."

How the Raskob Foundation brings different generations together

Patrick explains that the Raskob Foundation puts great emphasis on involving *every* member of the clan who wishes to participate.

"In our family foundation we have a saying that's at the core of what we do. It's that *every one* of the family members involved possesses a piece of the wisdom. What's important about that core belief is that it requires everyone to speak, and it levels the playing field. It also doesn't allow for grandstanding; it requires that those that may know more about a particular topic to share the stage."

This philosophy has proven effective for the Raskob Foundation, but it's reasonable to ask how other nonprofits—not based on familial connections—can adapt it for their own use. This is a vital lesson. When the relationship between nonprofits and for-profit businesses is managed right, it looks more like the Raskob Foundation—no grandstanding and a level playing field for ideas and projects used for mutual good and furtherance of a mission.

Patrick helps other families build their own legacy of generosity

Patrick McGrory is the chairperson of the Raskob Foundation, but it isn't his full-time job. He's also a private wealth advisor, helping his clients build and manage prosperity. Many of these do not have the benefit of a family legacy, introducing them to generosity at a young age. The best part of Patrick's job, he explains, is to fix that. He enables his clients to realize new philanthropic traditions they can one day hand down to future generations.

As he explains, "I hope on some level I provide witness, like my relatives did for me, to my clients. My goal is to truly inspire them to create a legacy of giving within their own families, as I have always had in my own." From our perspective, Patrick has seen the benefits of a Radical Connection his whole life. Nowadays, he's actively paying that mentality forward. By empowering his clients to find their own Radical Connections, he's fighting the Generosity Crisis one portfolio at a time, and we applaud him for it.

Bristol Myers Squibb Foundation: Building Trust and Community in Africa for Health Care Solutions

Bristol Myers Squibb is one of the leading global bio-pharmaceutical companies, creating lifesaving treatments for conditions as diverse as cancer, cardiovascular, and immunological diseases. It also funds a corporate foundation, which describes its grantmaking process this way: "At the Bristol Myers Squibb Foundation, we believe that geographic, economic, racial, or social circumstances should not determine health outcomes. We support that conviction with developing grantee relationships focused on cancers, cardiovascular disease, and immunologic disease in under-served communities and regions in the world that are less developed and heavily burdened."

Its emphasis on relationships isn't just lip service—it's the key to the foundation's success in addressing HIV/AIDS in sub-Saharan Africa over the past 20 years. The Bristol Myers Squibb Foundation launched its "Secure the Future" program in 1999 as a revolutionary approach to the massive epidemic. Guided by its mission of treating women and children with HIV in under-served areas, the program has funded 250 projects in 22 African countries, affecting millions of individuals in the two decades since its inception. We spoke with John Damonti, president of the Bristol Myers Squibb Foundation, vice president of corporate philanthropy and patient assistance, about the foundation's experiences and how it learned new strategies to successfully build community throughout Africa.

Was your foundation welcomed to Africa with open arms?

Unfortunately, no. It was quite a struggle to get started. When we launched the Secure the Future program, which was the first major private commitment for HIV/AIDS in Africa, it took more than a year for us to secure approval from the governments for our initial partnerships. Even though we were guided by a year of government consultations and had built local advisory boards to help develop our funding concepts and approval protocols we were met with great suspicion by in each of the five countries we launched in.

We weren't viewed as the Bristol Myers Squibb Foundation, an independent foundation trying to help with training and infrastructure, but perhaps more as a pharmaceutical company trying to create a market to sell HIV treatment to countries that simply couldn't afford them. The HIV epidemic on the continent was dire and it wasn't until we were able to form a strategic relationship with the health minister of Botswana that we were able to demonstrate what the power of public-private partnerships could deliver.

The country had the highest HIV infection rate in the world at 39% in the adult population (15 to 49 years old). We came to the health minister with three partnerships, one was to establish the first dedicated pediatric HIV program on the continent, the second, to help develop the country's first HIV reference laboratory, and third, a national psychosocial and education program. Once we began operating successfully in one country, it was soon after that *all* the other countries began to move forward with their proposed initiatives. Building trust takes time and we worked to ensure that everyone had a voice in the development of our initiatives. We also hired local staff from the five countries since this would not be a program run from New York, but a program run in Africa, by Africans for African solutions.

What was the biggest challenge your foundation faced in Africa?

We were among the first large funders coming onto the continent to help with the HIV epidemic. In the late 1990s and early 2000s there were huge challenges in the lack of affordable access to effective HIV medicines, along with appropriate trained health care practitioners to provide the care. All this was even more complicated by the fear and stigma that HIV brought to these communities so even running comprehensive testing programs was a challenge. We learned early on that we could have helped fund some very innovative approaches to help treat the disease in resource limited settings but if we didn't work to educate the community through both trusted traditional and non-traditional partners, the innovations would never gain traction.

At that time, we needed to invest heavily in community, working with traditional partners who were delivering roughly 80% of health care in the rural areas of Southern Africa: tribal leaders and chiefs, and most importantly, the community members themselves.

How did the foundation shift its focus to the community?

In the early 2000s, more funding materialized from multilateral and bilaterals and many more private funders for the operational side of medicine delivery. We therefore shifted much of our efforts to community building and mobilization. We entered into dialogue with traditional healers embracing what they effectively did for their patients, but also how HIV treatments could help save their patients' lives. We emphasized the importance of their role in treating opportunistic infections but, more importantly, ensuring that their patients should feel comfortable going to the treatment facilities to seek care. Forming a partnership instead of an adversarial relationship proved tremendously successful. Our approach reached deep into communities with faith-based organizations, people living with HIV, grandmothers, and the list goes on.

How has this success helped with other health problems in Africa?

By the late 2010s, after Secure the Future had been operating for more than 15 years in Africa, the United Nations noted that the continent's health challenges had shifted. People were no longer dying of AIDS in the large numbers they had been thanks to the success of large-scale treatment programs. As people lived longer, they were instead dying of non-communicable diseases such as diabetes, hypertension, and cancer.

As the Bristol Myers Squibb company moved out of HIV as a business, we saw this as an opportunity to leverage our insights and successes toward a new target. Essentially, we took everything we learned about the integration of community support and health systems and turned our attention to cancer. What we learned about treating women with HIV also applied to helping women with cancer, especially cervical cancer, which is so closely tied to HIV. Our advantage in moving to this new therapeutic area was facilitated by our 15-year history working with governments. This allowed us to enter the space as a trusted partner. Today, we are actively engaged in reducing deaths in nine countries in Africa, focused on cervical, lung, multiple myeloma, and pediatric cancers and blood disorders.

Has the community-driven aspect of your success in Africa been applied in other countries where the foundation works, including the US?

Our strategy with Secure the Future has influenced all the foundation's work in recent years, whether in China, Brazil, or the US. For one thing, we always emphasize the *community* approach in everything we do. For example, we've established a program aimed at increasing diversity in clinical trials by training 250 young investigators who are also racially and ethnically diverse or have a strong commitment to diversity in clinical trials. There's a second component exposing promising, underrepresented minority medical students to clinical trial research career pathways. Although this initiative is a diversion from our current health systems/community work, the program is built for the investigators to obtain two years of training on community integration because this is where the patients are who need to be recruited for clinical trials and where trust needs to be built.

As the renowned infectious diseases expert Dr. Richard Silvera explains, "Every clinical trial involves the unknown. Therefore, the currency for clinical trials is trust. Patients have to be able to trust that the researchers have their best interests in mind and are being transparent about what they are doing. And fostering that type of trust requires a real connection." The connection he describes in clinical trials is the very same type of connection we built over time in Africa. We view it as the best and most effective mechanism to create more diverse clinical trials, a benefit to all of humankind.

COMIC RELIEF US: HELPING CHILDREN ONE RED NOSE AT A TIME

Comic Relief US understands that generosity is a joyful act. For years, the mission-driven organization has applied this thinking to fighting poverty and creating a better future for children in the US and across the world. Of course, many other groups share this commitment, but Comic Relief US's approach is unique—it harnesses comedy and laughter to inspire action.

And inspire it has. The organization's signature "Red Nose Day" campaign raised a record $49 million in 2022 and in total, Comic Relief US has now brought in almost $380 million since launching in 2015. Comic Relief US uses these donations to invest in "both larger nonprofit and smaller community-led organizations with programs focused on tackling the root causes and consequences of poverty and social injustice. [They] support initiatives and policies that advance economic opportunity and leadership development in communities directly impacted by intergenerational poverty."

We sat down with Alison Moore, CEO of Comic Relief US, to discuss the success of Red Nose Day and how it works with its corporate partners.

Why do you think Red Nose Day has been such a successful campaign?

Comic Relief, and especially Red Nose Day, is all about harnessing the power of entertainment, levity, laughter, and joyfulness to create impact. For Red Nose Day, tapping into those happy emotions, plus the added silliness of red noses, creates a wonderful magic that we see every year. The red nose is an easy on-ramp to giving. Where normally a decision to give might involve six or seven steps from idea to action, the nose makes it a simple one- or two-step process. People think about the issue, see the nose, go with their gut (which is busy laughing), and act.

So, is giving a biological response to laughter and happiness? I'm not sure. Someone in a lab coat can verify that. What

I do know is that the results are so powerful, it is like catching lightning in a bottle. We combine key elements—our strong mission, our generous partners' collaboration, our innate creativity, our celebrity connections, the trust in our work—with the joy of levity. It creates a perfect storm of generosity when the magic of comedy and the red noses combine. From a fundraising side, a key partner collaboration is our incredible retail partnership with Walgreens.

What made Walgreens the right corporate partner for Comic Relief?

Red Nose Day had a record-breaking 2022 by achieving an amazing $49 million, across multiple channels. What is even more amazing is that over 60% of the money came from individual Walgreens customer donations. They were typically between $1 and $10 dollars, or even rounding up the sale to the next dollar.

The Walgreens partnership is an incredible example and shows the power of combining the magic of Red Nose Day with the power of a community-led brand like Walgreens. Consumers feel Red Nose Day in a different way when in store—enthusiastic employees, red branding, and red noses as a visual trigger—and, importantly, the feeling that their neighborhood store is a way to be in community together, and to do something good. Walgreens has a trusted partnership with their community. So when we introduced frictionless giving tools, like the key pad or round-up, it all came together to achieve our record-breaking campaign. Our messaging is also aligned. Red Nose Day's health work is centered around healthy outcomes for children with equitability and access as a strong through-line. Walgreens is also centered on health and has an emphasis on health equity and expanding health programs to everyone. Together we seek to build a healthy future for kids. This commonality makes the partnership feel natural, and our continued success together proves Walgreens customers see it the same way.

What's the major challenge to generosity and how do you fight it?

When Red Nose Day first came to the United States, it challenged people to think about issues through a very silly and humorous way. While it was a new approach for the US, it did connect with people's shorter attention spans. It made it easy. The philanthropy sector needs to continue to make it easy. Part of the Generosity Crisis is that giving has become hard—there are so many places to give, and there are so many issues to support—everyone is over-stimulated and bombarded with messaging. They worry, "Who should I support?" but when looking for inspiration, so little inspires them because of so much overstimulation.

The fun and levity of Red Nose Day cuts through that over-stimulation. But it can't just be holding a red nose—they also want to know where the money is going, what they are support-ing. As a result, we've created content that tells the story of our grantees and shows how Red Nose Day donations help kids enjoy a brighter future. These stories connect someone to how their donation is directly improving the lives of children. So our challenge is to combine the levity embedded in our brand and our marketing messages with the gravity of the issue and do so in a way that feels both entertaining, arresting, and provokes a desire to act now. It is a constant balance.

How can Comic Relief build on the success of Red Nose Day?

A just world free from poverty is our vision and breaking the cycle of intergenerational poverty is our North Star. The list of things we could focus on to contribute to that vision is almost endless. So, to create an anchored focus, we have four main pillars: safety, health, education, and empowerment. Red Nose Day encompasses all pillars, but will increasingly create additional breadth: children's health, aligned with our Walgreens partnership. We trust that in the future we will find partners who are equally interested in supporting issues related to safety, education, and empowerment. In partnership, we can build new campaigns and experiences in which we can galvanize customers and employees to act and start to create a new giving platform for the partner—like we have created with Walgreens and Red Nose Day. The most important part is to produce the magic that breaks down barriers, leverages the power of entertainment and levity, and creates momentum for giving. As we proved in 2022, with the right partner, Red Nose Day inspires great acts of generosity. And we expect more good things to come.

*****

As we explained in the beginning of this book, generosity's future is not at all ensured. Today's forms of charitable giving are taking on novel and unprecedented forms, challenging traditional notions of philanthropy. Moving forward, if all of us don't demand authentic relationships over transactions for the common good—and if we allow philanthropy to be the sum of transactional activities—generosity as we've known it will soon collapse.

The material presented in this book is meant to be a wake-up call and a call to action. Zoos, museums, the arts, and so many other wonderful things that make life worthwhile depend on others' good will. Likewise, essential services, such as hospitals, shelters, and food pantries, providing for our most vulnerable, will find themselves in dire jeopardy should present conditions continue—and/or worsen.

In the US, we are long accustomed to incredible affluence scarcely imaginable in previous historical periods. Unfortunately, as beneficiaries of such a largesse we have little contextual appreciation as to just how good we have it. A failure of imagination prevents us from appreciating just what it would be like to lose so many mainstays we've come to expect as our American birthright.

Again, tomorrow's beneficence is *not* guaranteed. The past doesn't presage the future. It can all go away. Yet, such uncertainty also heralds potentially good news. We can (re)write our destiny. In service of this dream, let this book serve as an awareness-building tool. Let it also catalyze needed action. Before it's too late.

The first step is to (re)embrace "love of people." For too long, negative feelings like indifference and even hostility have poisoned our interpersonal relations, especially through atomizing tech. Alone, peering into our endless screens, we have hardened our hearts toward our brothers and sisters. Technologically rich, we have become emotionally poor.

This can change, too.

It begins by a recognition that philanthropy in all forms requires two parties. By shifting our values toward building *and* rebuilding meaningful relationships—Radical Connections—we can reverse our Generosity Crisis. We can solve humanity's greatest challenges. The stories we have presented throughout this book demonstrate what's possible when we marry the theoretical with the practical. It's our hope that so many people and organizations' passion to change the status quo strengthens your own resolve to restore our nation's giving traditions. More than anything, we hope we have inspired you.

It's been our privilege to bring this information to you. Please let it be the final push you need to act now. For the good of all.

INDEX